THE PULLMAN STRIKE

by
William H. Carwardine

**Introduction by
Virgil J. Vogel**

**Biographical note on Carwardine
by William Adelman**

**1973
Chicago
Charles H. Kerr & Company**

Published for the Illinois Labor History Society

Printed in the United States of America

LC 73-77550

ISBN 0-88286-003-8

TABLE OF CONTENTS

LIST OF ILLUSTRATIONS

Rev. William H. Carwardine
Pastor of the First M.E. Church, Pullman Ill.

I

KING DEBS.

Pullman Strikers at the Main Gate
Courtesy of Chicago Historical Society

III

Troopers on the Grounds of the Florence Hotel

Courtesy of Chicago Historical Society

IV

INTRODUCTION

by Virgil J. Vogel

I. Background

When the 31 year old Rev. William Carwardine, pastor of the Methodist church at Pullman, wrote his little book on the Pullman strike, that epochal battle was still raging. The workers at Pullman went out on May 11, 1894, and the Pullman car boycott, which quickly became a strike on the major railroads, began on June 26. During this time, it appears, the Rev. Carwardine twice met Eugene Debs, president of the American Railway Union. Debs testified at his conspiracy trial in January, 1895, that he had visited Pullman on May 14 and 18 and talked with Rev. Carwardine about conditons there. (Karsner, 1919, p. 145). Also, during June, Karsner relates, "Rev. Carwardine addressed the A.R.U. Convention, told of the living conditions of the workers of Pullman, and pleaded with the convention to 'act quickly in the name of God and humanity.'" (*Ibid.* p. 146). What sort of help he had in mind is unclear, because in his book he says that he did not endorse the strike and boycott (p. 118), but felt that it was justified by conditions.

Mr. Carwardine must have begun his book about this time, for the launching of the boycott is mentioned early, and on page 38 he gives the date of "the present writing" as July 23. The exact date that it was finished, and when it came off the press with the Kerr imprint, is not known, but it could not have been more than two weeks later. Mr. John H. Driver's introduction to it is dated July 30, and the book does not mention the special convention of the ARU which met on August 2d to consider the bitter fact of defeat. When the United States Strike Commission (USSC), appointed by President Grover Cleveland, met at Chicago on August 15, this book was already circulating, and the commission heard testimony from Rev. Carwardine on the

17th. His remarks fill ten pages of the Commission's report, and consist mostly of his replies to questions about the statements made in this book. It appears likely, therefore, that the actual writing of this 126 page book occupied no more than four weeks, although his fact gathering doubtless began sooner.

The haste in which it was written in no way impairs its credibility or its factual reliability. Rev. Carwardine was a humanitarian and a brave man, challenging one of the most stubborn tyrants of his age, because he could not remain indifferent to the callous treatment of the workmen in his community. The price of his boldness was exile from Pullman in September, 1894, after three years in residence there.

Carroll Wright, U.S. Commissioner of Labor, was one of his interrogators, as chairman of the USSC. Ten years earlier, Mr. Wright had toured Pullman and enthusiastically endorsed its concept. He enjoyed a free pass for the use of Pullman cars. Wright questioned Mr. Carwardine rather closely about his political philosophy, a procedure which would seem alien to his fact gathering mission. After Carwardine declared that employers should be "more just toward their employees," the following ensued:

Com. Wright: Do you carry these views far enough to advocate what is known as state socialism as a way out of the present difficulties?

Ans. I am not prepared to take that position.

Com. Wright: You have not advocated it yet? Ans. No sir; I have not. I do not like to commit myself to the policy as yet, but I confess I am inclined very much toward some of these things.

Com. Wright: You have been charged with being both a socialist and an anarchist? Ans. Yes sir.

Com. Wright: You of course understand the difference in the terms?

Ans. Yes sir.

Com. Wright: And if you are a socialist you can not be an anarchist at the same time? Ans. Yes sir.

Com. Wright: How much truth is there in that

public charge?
Ans. In regard to anarchy?
Com. Wright: Yes sir. Ans. That charge would be so low that I really don't feel like answering it; to suppose for a moment that I, who am American born, my father a soldier who died for his country— to suppose that I for one moment would be thought an anarchist is to me one of the most contemptible and false charges that could possibly be brought against me. I might be what you would call a Christian socialist, but as to anarchy, I repudiate it entirely.
Com. Wright: I thought it fair to allow you to define your position relative to these difficulties, and that is why I asked the question.
Ans. I confess I am surprised at the prejudice which exists on the part of a great many people toward this whole matter. I am told that my book has not been read because people believe I am of that tendency, and I know that my publisher [Charles H. Kerr] has endeavored to get certain publishing agencies to take my book and sell it and they have said: "It is a good book, what we in the phrase of the business call 'a seller,' but we prefer not to handle it." I simply refer to that as showing the intense prejudice against literature of this kind. But my brethren in the clergy do not all agree with me in the position I occupy, and I wish to say this: I was a clergyman in the town of Pullman and had to do one of two things. I had to keep quiet and say nothing, and at the same time realize that these men were not being rightly treated, or else I had to speak out my convictions, and that is the reason I have been interested as a clergyman in this matter. (USSC, pp. 448-49).

The commissioners seemed also to be trying to shake the evidence in Rev. Carwardine's book, but only in one detail did they cause him to retreat slightly. When his statement on page 98 of this book, that housing as good as that in Pullman could be rented in adjoining communities for 20 percent less rent, was questioned by one of the commissioners, Rev. Carwardine conceded that perhaps the figure should be closer to 15 percent, if allowance was made for Pullman's much vaunted "sanitation, etc." It appears however that Carwardine's original figures actually understated the difference, rather than exaggerating it. Real estate agents and competent witnesses set the difference as high as 25 percent, and this figure was cited by the commission itself in its report.

Pullman's second vice-president, Thomas Wickes, devoted much of his time before the USSC to challenging Rev. Carwardine's facts and figures. In determining whom to believe, one must consider that on one hand is the actual manager of the Pullman empire, wholly devoted to the selfish interests of his chief, and on the other a fearless man whose sole motive was sympathy for the suffering workmen who were in his flock. None of the scholarly works about the Pullman strike which have since appeared has upset Carwardine's testimony.

Carwardine's book is a valuable collection of facts about social and economic conditions in the Pullman community in 1894. It is a brief on behalf of working people's rights, an argument which in that day seldom came from respectable quarters. As a history of the Pullman strike, however, it is inadequate. The prior history of the Pullman company and its company town, the sympathy boycott and strike which tied up virtually all railroads west of Chicago, are barely mentioned. The manner of the strike's ending, and its aftermath, the prosecution of Debs and his fellow union officers on contempt and conspiracy charges, are not dealt with because they were still in the future. To fill these gaps, it was decided to provide this new introduction, and a bibliography.

In evaluating this book, it is also necessary to say that whenever Rev. Carwardine enters the realm of theory, he shows naivete. It is a fault for which he can be forgiven, for it is more than redeemed by the deep humanism that inspires this account. But, just as he could not "endorse" the strike, while he did everything to help the hungry, so there is incongruity in his belief in a common ground for capital and labor, and his remark: "If they are to exist at all, they must live as husband and wife, each the counterpart of each other, each for the other's interest and welfare." Debs, in contrast, while not yet a socialist in name, attacked the "wage system" and declared that he saw no solution to industrial troubles under the existing system. (USSC, P. 169).

II. History of Pullman

George M. Pullman was a mechanic's son, born in a small New York town in 1831. His schooling ended at fourteen when he began working as a cabinet maker. He later became involved in several profitable business undertakings, and for part of the Civil War years, he was in the Colorado gold fields. For reasons not clear, Pullman, like a dozen other contemporaries who were to become wealthy tycoons—including Carnegie, Gould and Rockefeller—managed to avoid service in that bloody affair.

Before the war ended Pullman began to develop an improved sleeping car and attracted attention by attaching one of his cars to Abraham Lincoln's funeral train. In 1867 Pullman incorporated the Pullman Palace Car Co. under Illinois law. The company was authorized to purchase, manufacture, sell, and operate railway cars and own such real estate as might be necessary to the operation of the business. Its capitalization was a million dollars. By the time of the Pullman strike the company was to have a capitalization of $36 million, and assets valued at twice that amount, plus an undivided surplus of $25 million, mostly coined out of the sweat of Pullman's workers in 27 years. The number of stockholders grew to 4,000, of which Marshall Field was a prominent and influential member. Pullman maintained in 1894 that he did not own a controlling interest, but however that may be, he did in fact control the operations of the company. Policy decisions were his.

Early in 1880 George Pullman decided to build his main plant and a model company town near Chicago. (Other plants, in 1894, were at Detroit, St. Louis, Ludlow, Ky., and Wilmington, Del.) Through an intermediary, James H. Bowen, he began secretly to purchase land on the west shore of Lake Calumet, a shallow body of water just south of Chicago. In a few months he had acquired 75 parcels totalling 4,000 acres of land 6¼ square miles, for $800,000, or an average of $200 per acre. In 1892 the land was valued at $5 million, an increase of over 600 percent in a dozen years. Pullman's lots alone, 25 x 125 feet, though not for sale, were valued at $200 each. And every foot of this land, even after development, was classified for tax purposes as "farm land." Pullman maintained that the community he established received few services from the village of Hyde Park, of which it was politically a part, or the city of Chicago, to which it was annexed, over Pullman's strenuous objections, in 1889. Yet his stubborn refusal to negotiate, mediate, or arbitrate his differences with his employees was to create in 1894 a major financial burden on the city and state, and the general public, in terms of pay for police and national guard protection, and the financial losses created by a strike due to his intransigence.

Solon Beman, who designed Pullman's $300,000 mansion at 1729 South Prairie Avenue in Chicago, was employed as principal architect for the town of Pullman. A city which was eventually to house over 12,000 people was quickly built simultaneously with the construction of the plant. Row houses for workers' families predominated, with some tenement apartments for single persons, and a few expensive dwellings for management and professional people. Every home and every building and shop, even the church, remained company property, and were rented to the tenants. One worker reportedly said "We are born in a Pullman house, fed from the Pullman shop, taught in the Pullman school, catechized in the Pullman church, and when we die we shall be buried in the Pullman cemetery and go to the Pullman hell." (Ginger, p. 110). By such total control, Pullman maintained, he could keep out saloons and other enterprises which were harmful to his workers. Only in the Florence Hotel, named for his eldest daughter, could liquor be obtained, and only by those who could afford to go there.

Pullman town was an example of industrial feudalism on a grand scale. It was a patriarchal institution straight from the Middle Ages. It was a company town completely controlled by the corporation which was the sole employer and landowner. Yet there were, among visitors who came to view it, many who regarded it as a marvelous example of philanthropy. Pullman himself, however, made it clear that the town was intended to yield a profit, just as the car works, of not less than 6 percent. Even the library charged an annual fee of $3 and the single church building was for rent at such a high figure that it remained vacant for long periods.

It is a commentary on the living conditions of workers generally at that time that observers found much to admire at Pullman. They praised it for its lawns, trees, and flowers, its cleanliness, its pleasing architecture, its community institutions, and its healthfulness. Yet the houses were, and are still, packed closely together with only very small yards. The streets for the most part follow the dismal gridiron pattern of the cities. There were also cheap wooden shacks in the brickyards which were not shown to visitors. Even the brick homes had no bathroom and only one inside water tap. The worst aspect of life in Pullman was that the lives and behavior of the residents were under constant surveillance, through a spy system. Leases could be terminated on ten days notice, and tenants were responsible for all repairs and most of the maintenance. Although the lease did not allow it, many tenants took in boarders and roomers in order to make ends meet.

Professor Richard T. Ely, the economist, wrote an article on Pullman for *Harper's Weekly* in 1885 which was a mixture of praise and criticism. "In a hundred ways," he wrote, "one sees in Pullman today evidences of his founder's sagacious foresight." He pointed out that the death rate was about half that in the rest of the town of Hyde Park. He completely overlooked the fact that the age distribution of Pullman's inhabitants was much lower than in other places. The Pullman Company hired mostly young workers, and there were simply no aged or retired people in the town. It is no surprise therefore that the statistics would show a low death rate, yet Ely and others failed to note the reasons. Moreover, the death rate by 1894 had risen to that of Hyde Park, about 15 per 1000.

Prof. Ely shortsightedly conceded that Mr. Pullman had "partially solved one of the great problems of the immediate present, which is a diffusion of the benefits of concentrated wealth among wealth-creators." How wide of the mark this judgement was became evident in the strike of 1894.

Even Jane Addams of Hull House persisted in seeing Pullman as a model of philanthropy, despite Pullman's own insistence that it was nothing of the kind. While deploring his paternalism and his intransigence toward the union, she wrote that "he alone gave his men so model a town, such perfect surroundings." ("A Modern Lear," in Ginger, *American Social Thought,* p. 191).

Prof. Ely's general conclusions about Pullman were generally unfavorable on humanistic grounds. "The power of Bismarck in German is utterly insignificant," he charged, "when compared with the power of the ruling authority of the Pullman Palace Car Company in Pullman." He complained that the town had no newspaper "through which complaint might find utterance," and "not one single resident dare speak out openly his opinion about the town in which he lives. One feels that one is mingling with a dependent, servile people." The citizen was "surrounded by constant restraint and restriction, and everything done for him, nothing by him." He charged that the Pullman system was "un-American." It was "benevolent, well-wishing feudalism," and if the system should spread, it would bring "the establishment of the most absolute power of capital, and the repression of all freedom." These sentiments were in accord with those of Rev. Carwardine, who called Pullman "a sort of hollow mockery, a sham, an institution girdled with red tape," and a "civilized relic of European serfdom."

III Genesis of the Strike

The Pullman Company prospered, and by the time of the World's Columbian Exposition at Chicago in 1893, according to George M. Pullman, the company was capitalized at 36 million, contrasted to the million with which it began, and its properties were actually valued at twice that amount. It had an undivided surplus of 25 million. Moreover, during the three years preceding the strike, and during the strike, the company regularly paid its 4,000 stockholders dividends at a rate of not less than 8 percent per annum. From 1868 to 1894, Pullman reported that dividend payments totalled $28,554,347.50. Much of these capital gains, and all of these profits, were coined out of the exploitation of Pullman's workers, who enriched the Pullman company not only through their low wages, but also in the high rents they paid, and the profits made on gas, water, and even the Pullman bank.

In the fall of 1893 a general economic recession set in and the Pullman Company, according to testimony Mr. Pullman later gave to the U.S. Strike Commission, was compelled to bid on car building contracts at less than cost in order to keep its workers employed. To survive, Mr. Pullman argued, it became necessary to cut wages an average of 25 percent, and to lay off many workers. Since wages were barely at the subsistence level beforehand, destitution soon followed. Meanwhile, the workers were required to pay the same high rents as before. Testimony to the strike commission revealed that workers were afraid to seek cheaper lodgings elsewhere, because the company gave employment preference to Pullman residents. To obtain and protect their jobs, they were virtually required to live in Pullman houses, according to the testimony of Thomas Heathcote, chairman of the strike committee at Pullman. (USSC, p. 425)

Pullman also maintained that the question of the rents was completely unrelated to the problem of the Pullman plant, even though nearly all the residential housing was owned by the Pullman Palace Car Company.

In view of the low price Pullman paid for the land, the low taxes, and the economics of large scale construction, it can be calculated from Pullman's own figures that the entire cost of a Pullman house was recovered from rents in about four years—a return of 25 percent.

Another interesting facet of the economic picture at Pullman is that wage and staff reductions, as well as short time, were for workers only; there were no cuts in managerial salaries or personnel, and there were no reductions in dividends. Moreover, there was a rent reduction for Pullman shopkeepers (USSC, pp. 507-508). In other words, the entire burden of any financial setbacks caused by the business recession were expected to be borne by the workers alone, not shared by management or stockholders.

Still another fact that has received little attention in writings about the Pullman strike is that the Pullman Company had both a manufacturing division and an operating division. The latter division leased sleeping cars to the railroads, and hired the porters who worked in them. The profits of the operating division were not seriously affected by the decline in the building of freight cars, ordinary coaches, street cars, etc., and helped overcome the very slight manufacturing losses.

Pullman declared that he lost $50,000 producing cars below cost, yet a dividend of twelve times that amount was declared two days after the strike began. If dividends had been cut to 6 percent, it has been estimated, none of the wage cuts would have been necessary. Pullman declared that the average employee earned $600 a year, before the cuts. With 4,000 workers employed, this made a wage bill of $2,400,000. Since quarterly dividends of $600,000 were being paid, the annual total of dividends was about equal to the wage bill. Therefore, all the trouble at Pullman could have been avoided if dividends had been reduced from 8 percent to 6 percent, saving $480,000 a year. Alternately, Pullman could have dipped into the huge undivided surplus, without in any way imperiling the company.

Still another relevant item is that the manufacturing division of Pullman car works had two major divisions: construction and repair. While construction orders were down in the winter of 1893-94, the repair work continued at its former pace. One worker wrote to Carwardine that from the fall of 1893 on, repair work constituted three fourths of the work done. (p. 103, herein). There would seem to be no reason, therefore, why wages should be cut in the repair division, except that given by Pullman's second vice-president, Thomas H. Wickes, in explaining why the company did not volunteer to raise wages when business was good: "We go into the market for men, just as we go into the market for anything else, and the Pullman Company...would be expected to pay the market price for labor, the same as any other manufacturers." (Thomas Heathcote, chairman of the Pullman strikers, charged that Pullman paid $1.90 a day for repair work, while railroads were paying $2.50). In this labor market of which Mr. Wickes spoke, arguments based on justice, productivity or company earnings stop no wage cut; concerted refusal to work, or the threat of it, has often raised wages or stopped cuts, but even then only to the extent that the market made possible. For this reason unionists who see that market as clearly as Mr. Wickes did aim in some way to replace the capitalist labor market by arrangements under which their capacity to work is no longer a commodity.

Suffering was widespread in Pullman in the Spring of 1894. Piece rates were cut, and hours were reduced, so that wages of $9 a week were common, and many workers found themselves unable to pay their rents. (Formerly the rents were deducted from wages, until this practice was outlawed by the legislature. Then the company made out two checks,—as described on page 69—one for rent, the other for wages above the rent, and workers were pressured to sign over the first check at the bank window).

Thomas W. Heathcote, chairman of the Pullman ARU locals, later told the strike commission:

> I have known men to drop down by the side of a car when they were working for want of food, and the way I had to work myself, in order to make the amount of money I did (about $20 a month), I would frequently have to sit down at 10 o'clock in order to rest until I got strength to go on again, and there were hundreds of men in that condition at the Pullman shops when we quit.

He also testified that he had "seen men with families of eight or nine children to support crying there (at the pay window) because they only got 3 or 4 cents after paying their rents; I have seen them stand by the window and cry for enough money to keep their families; I have been insulted at that window time and time again by the clerks when I tried to get money enough to support my family, even after working every day and overtime."

It was during this period that many of the 3300 workers still employed at Pullman began to organize into locals of the American Railway Union. The ARU was an industrial union organized in June of 1893 for the purpose of overcoming the craft division which kept rail workers disunited and weak. Under the intelligent and aggressive leadership of its president,

Eugene V. Debs, the new union soon won a strike against the Great Northern Railroad, which caused its membership to zoom until it reached 150,000, a large figure for those days.

Enemies of the union, including President Cleveland, maintained that it was "improper" for the ARU to organize Pullman employees, because they were not railway workers. Defenders (Howard, USSC, p. 15) responded that since the Pullman company operated trains on a few miles of track serving its own plant, that all Pullman workers were railroad employees under the industrial union concept and the provisions of the ARU constitution.

There were nineteen locals of the ARU, representing different departments, organized at the Pullman works, which chose a committee of 46 to meet with management to discuss grievances, which included not only the wage cuts and piece work speedup, but also grievances against foreman. At first they did not receive access to the august presence of Mr. Pullman, but met with Mr. Thomas Wickes on May 7 and May 9, and were briefly addressed by Mr. Pullman at the second meeting. Their demands for restoration of the wage scales prevailing in the summer of 1893 were rejected. Mr. Pullman himself told the committee that wages could not be restored because of economic conditions, but he promised to investigate complaints against foremen, and shop conditions. The next day, in violation of a promise made by Mr. Pullman, three members of the committee were fired.

ARU representatives, and even the Pullman local chairman, Thomas Heathcote, advised against a strike at the all-night meeting of local representatives held at nearby Kensington on the night of May 10, but the sentiment to go out was too overwhelming to be restrained. According to Carwardine they voted to strike May 12, although Heathcote said no date was set. On the morning of May 11 rumors circulated that the management, informed of union plans by a spy, was planning a lockout, whereupon the word was passed to walk out at once. As hundreds began leaving, Pullman did close the plant and notices were posted to that effect. The historic Pullman strike began.

IV Progress of the Strike and Boycott

Immediate measures to protect the Pullman property were taken by the union, which posted 300 pickets, called "guards," to forestall possible vandalism. So well disciplined were the strikers, however, that not a single act of property damage occurred in Pullman throughout the strike. So strongly were the men dedicated to sobriety and order, that a casual observer could scarcely be aware that a great social struggle was going on, until troops camped in front of the Florence Hotel on Independence Day. The violence which broke out elsewhere, about seven weeks after the strike began, was not attributable to the strikers.

ARU President Debs toured the Pullman community on May 14, and talked with the striking workers. On the 18th he talked with Rev. Carwardine and Jennie Curtiss, a seamstress and leader of the women workers at Pullman.

On June 9 the ARU national convention met at Uhlich's hall in Chicago, and it was addressed on June 12 by the Rev. Carwardine who urged them to help the Pullman workers. On the 15th a written address from the Pullman workers was read. In addition to grievances already described, it complained:

> Water which Pullman buys from the city at 8 cents a thousand gallons he retails to us at 500 per cent advance and claims he is losing $400 a month on it. Gas which sells at 75 cents per thousand feet in Hyde Park, just north of us, he sells for $2.25. When we went to tell him our grievances he said we were all his "children."

> Pullman, both the man and the town, is an ulcer on the body politic...George M. Pullman, you know, has cut our wages from 30 to 70 per cent. George M.

Pullman has caused to be paid in the last year the regular quarterly dividend of 2 per cent on his stock and an extra slice of 1½ per cent, making 9½ per cent (annual rate) on $30,000,000 of capital.

The address also claimed that Pullman absorbed small losses in the manufacturing division only because that was cheaper than losing men. "We will make you proud of us brothers," read the address, "if you will give us the hand we need." (USSC pp. 87-89).

The convention appointed a committee consisting of both Pullman workers and convention delegates who were not employed at Pullman, to seek a meeting with Mr. Wickes to ask for arbitration of the dispute at Pullman. Mr. Wickes declared that he would not meet with anybody from the ARU, as such, but only with Pullman employees. The committee was then reconstituted to consist of Pullman workers only. This committee then asked of Mr. Wickes that the issues be submitted to arbitration, but he only reiterated the position of Mr. Pullman that "there is nothing to arbitrate." He also refused to arbitrate the question whether there was anything to arbitrate. (Mr. Pullman, soon after the strike began, left Chicago with his family for his seashore home at Long Branch, N.J., and remained there until it was over.)

In consequence of this stubborn reaction, the convention declared on June 21 that unless the Pullman company agreed to arbitration within 5 days, ARU members would refuse to handle trains containing Pullman sleeping cars. The delegates received instructions by wire from their locals and approved this action unanimously.

The Pullman Company received the support of the General Managers Association, an organization representing 24 railroads terminating at Chicago, formed a few years earlier for the purpose of presenting a common front on wage demands. During the Pullman strike, it also became a scab recruiting agency, setting up offices in the East for that purpose. At a full meeting, attended by Mr. Wickes, the GMA voted unanimously to resist the ARU boycott and to continue handling Pullman cars.

Workers who refused to handle Pullman cars on June 26 were fired, whereupon the boycott was transformed into a strike. The nationwide boycott and strike proved effective, especially at Chicago and in the states to the West. Trains with Pullman cars were not moved unless the cars were disconnected. The union charged that the companies tried to attach Pullman cars to trains that did not normally carry them, in order to be able to claim that the mails were being interfered with. There is little doubt that the ARU could have brought the railroads to their knees and caused them to pressure Pullman to negotiate or arbitrate, were it not for the intervention of the federal government. Eugene Debs declared that "up to the first day of July, or after the strike had been in progress five days, the railway managers, as we believed, were completely defeated. Their immediate resources were exhausted, their properties were paralyzed, and they were unable to operate their trains." (USSC, p. 142).

Debs maintained that the partisan actions of President Grover Cleveland (whom Debs had supported in three campaigns) and the federal courts saved the employers from defeat. Cleveland, on the advice of attorney general Richard Olney, a former railroad attorney, appointed a special federal counsel to deal with the strike, in the person of Edwin Walker, who was at that time, and had been for 24 years, counsel for the Milwaukee Railroad. The brazen conflict of interest represented by this appointment raised no eyebrows outside the labor movement.

It was Walker who recruited some 4,000 U.S. deputy marshals whose ostensible purpose was to preserve law and order, but who actually served in many instances as strike breakers. Whenever railroad men were fired for boycotting Pullman cars, their scab replacements were sworn in as deputy marshals, and given a gun and badge, while receiving their pay from the railroads. Thus, the federal government gave up its pretense of impartiality in this class struggle. Other deputy marshals played the role of agent provocateur and encouraged acts of vandalism and destruction. They were recruited from among criminal elements and saloon habitues. Many of them engaged in acts of looting railroad cars, and intimidating and brutalizing strikers and sympathizers. Several dozen of them had to be arrested by the Chicago police for lawless acts. Police chief Michael Brennan of Chicago reported that they were "more in the way than of any service. Not only that, but the police force frequently had occasion to restrain them and arrest them for indiscriminate shooting." (USSC, p. 355).

The mayor of Chicago, John P. Hopkins, was a Democrat, a resident of Pullman, a former employee of the Pullman company, and a grocer and dry goods merchant. His sympathies were on the side of the workers, and the police, with some exceptions, did not often engage, during this trike, in such acts of anti-labor violence as characterized their behavior in the historic encounters at Haymarket in 1886 or the Memorial Day massacre in 1937. In fact, as Carwardine's book indicates, the police even contributed money and goods for strike relief.

Management witnesses charged later before the strike commission that the police did not do their duty. Everett St. John, chairman of the GMA, alleged that police did not interfere with people blocking passage of an engine at 52d street on the 4th of July. (USSC, p. 216). Mayor Hopkins replied that "our police force did their duty, but I could not say but what some of the policemen were in sympathy with the strikers; I presume they were, and I am free to admit, so far as the Pullman strikers were concerned, I was with them myself." (USSC, p. 348). Police and state militia fired into a crowd of people at 49th and Loomis on July 7, killing three, and wounding an undetermined number. Police also killed a woman spectator the same day at the Northwestern tracks and Ashland Avenue.

Still, the strike commission was sufficiently alarmed

at the possiblity that law and order might collapse because of divided loyalties that they declared in their report:

> That policemen sympathized with strikers rather than the corporations can not be doubted, nor would it be surprising to find the same sentiment rife among the military. These forces are largely recruited from the laboring classes. Indeed, the danger is growing that in strike wars between corporations and employers, military duty will ultimately have to be done by others than volunteers from labor ranks. (USSC, p. xliv).

Mayor Hopkins tried to intercede with the Pullman Company to settle the strike, but was rebuffed at every attempt. After the intervention of federal troops, he sought to deliver a message from the ARU to the GMA offering to call off the strike if the strikers, except for any accused of violence, were rehired. The message was returned with the remark that the GMA did not wish to receive any communication from the ARU. John Egan, GMA manager, was reported in the press as saying that the mayor should not be a "messenger boy" for the union. Later, Mr. Worthington of the USSC asked Mr. Egan if there was anything in the document that was offensive or insulting. Egan answered evasively and arrogantly: "I considered that any party who attacked railway companies as the American Railway Union had done, and were whipped, as I considered they were, it was displaying considerable cheek to dictate the terms of their surrender." (USSC, p. 271).

V Federal Intervention

The first instances of forcible action to interfere with the passage of trains apparently occurred not in Chicago, but in the southwestern suburb of Blue Island, which contains the yards of the Rock Island Railroad, a company which bore the brunt of the strike and boycott. This railroad, unlike the others, was joint owner of the

Pullman cars on its trains, instead of a mere lessee. A meeting was held at Blue Island on the night of June 29, which was addressed by Debs and ARU vice-president George P. Howard. Only about half of the hundreds present, according to reports, were railroad men. Both union leaders counselled non-violence, but Howard allegedly called Pullman a son of a bitch. The men voted to strike the Rock Island line next morning at 7 A.M. According to Everett St. John, general manager of the Rock Island and chairman of the GMA, coaches were switched on to through tracks to block trains. A local suburban train (not carrying mail) was stopped at Blue Island the evening of June 20 because of blocked tracks. According to St. John:

An effort was made to clear the tracks to get these trains out, but was unsuccessful on account of the interference of the mob, who stoned the engineer and dragged the fireman from his engine. Matters were further complicated by city authorities at Blue Island who were in sympathy with the mob, and arrested road master while making the attempt to clear the tracks. (USSC, p. 214).

According to testimony most of the crowds at Blue Island were composed, not of railroad men, but of townspeople and workers from a nearby brickyard. One was even identified as a detective. Several reporters so testified, and were not contradicted. It was also pointed out that ARU men tried to disperse these crowds.

On July 2 United States Marshal John Arnold with about 125 men left Chicago about 7 A.M., reaching Blue Island about 9:30. Then, according to St. John of the GMA:

...an attempt was made to clear east bound suburban track. The mob resisted every attempt to do this, in which they were aided by police of Blue Island. In order to reach the cars obstructing the track it was necessary to cross Vermont Street. The mob stopped a team on track to prevent the passage of engine, and when driver drove out the way his team was seized and again turned on to the crossing. They threw themselves in front of the coaches, which was in advance of engine, and by every means in their power tried to prevent engine backing up. Blue Island police stood with their watches in their hands ready to arrest the crew of engine as soon as five minutes allowed by ordinance, during which a crossing may be blocked, was exceeded. Attempt was also made by the police to arrest U.S. Marshal Arnold, which was resisted by him. After a riot, in which pistols were drawn, and Deputy U.S. Marshal John A. Logan was stabbed by one of the rioters, the mob was driven back and two coaches were taken off the main track. Track was still obstructed, however, by other cars. After this it was not thought advisable to make another attempt until more force was provided. Marshal Arnold called on District Attorney Milchrist for U.S. troops to assist him in protecting trains, and Deputy Sheriff Leibrandt also made request for state troops. (USSC, p. 215).

Although the ARU deplored such disturbances, and in fact even instructed its people to report rioters to the authorities, on July 2 a federal injunction was issued by Judge William A. Woods, under the Sherman anti-trust act of 1890, forbidding the ARU from "compelling or inducing, by threats, intimidations, persuasion, force or violence, railway employees to refuse or fail to perform their duties." Thus a law supposedly designed to control big business was transformed by the courts into an anti-labor weapon.

The same day Walker, Cleveland's strike counsel, advised the president that U.S. troops would be required to enforce the orders of the court and protect the transportation of mail. It is noteworthy that up to this point there were no acts of violence in Chicago, and only a few elsewhere. The strike commission testimony shows that violence was precipitated by the calling out of the federal troops and U.S. marshals. Their function was not to avert violence, but to defeat a strike which.

up to that time, was victorious and peaceful. Except for the incidents at Blue Island, trains did not move because men would not work on them. Debs later remarked that it was not the armed forces, however, which broke the strike, but the courts.

The president responded at once to Walker's advice, and had his military chief, Gen. J. M. Schofield, issue orders to Gen. Nelson Miles to transport the entire Ft. Sheridan garrison to Chicago. (It is interesting that the officer chosen to command the troops at Chicago was the same one who received the surrender of Chief Joseph of the Nez Perce tribe on October 5, 1877, and who commanded the troops sent to supress the "ghost dance troubles" among the Sioux, which culminated in the Wounded Knee massacre, December 29, 1890. At one point in Chicago, Miles asked for permission to fire on crowds. It appears, however, that militia, marshals, and police did most of the actual shooting).

The troops sent to Chicago were only one contingent. Others were dispatched to many points in the West where the strike was spectacularly effective, and the total number of federal troops called out numbered over 12,000, or about one half of the entire standing army of the U.S. at that time.

Governor John P. Altgeld, also a Democrat, and a humane and decent man, sent some 2,000 militia to Chicago, at the suggestion of Mayor Hopkins on July 6, and strongly protested to the president against the presence of federal troops in Chicago. He maintained that they were not needed, and their dispatch was a violation of the constitution (Art. IV, sec 4) which provides that the U.S. may protect a state against "domestic violence" only on application of the legislature or the executive, and neither of these conditions was met. Cleveland based his action on an obscure law (Sec. 5298 Rev. Stat.) passed during reconstruction days to put down the Ku Klux Klan. (It was next used by President Eisenhower to enforce integration at Little Rock in 1956).

Ten years later, in a self-serving address at

Princeton University, Cleveland accused the governor, then deceased, of having contributed to the "annoyances" of 1894 by his behavior, and dismissed his legal arguments as "rather dreary discussion of the importance of preserving the rights of the states."

The report of the U.S. Strike Commission, appointed by Cleveland, declared, "It is in evidence, and uncontradicted, that no violence or destruction of property by strikers or sympathizers took place at Pullman, and that until July 3 (when federal troops arrived at Chicago) no extraordinary protection was had from the police and military against even anticipated disorder." Chicago police chief Michael Brennan also told the commission that "no serious riot or violence had occurred up to that time (July 3), and the police force had been handling it for ten days." (USSC, p. 354).

The presence of the troops and the marshals, sworn in just before their arrival, changed all that. Thousands of strike sympathizers, many wearing the white ribbons that Debs had asked union men to wear, rose in fury and began to react by blocking trains, upsetting cars and even engines, and setting fire to rolling stock. On July 3d tracks were blocked and rolling stock, including a locomotive, were upset at Blue Island, on the Rock Island tracks. A federal marshal with 100 deputies arrived there and tried to read the federal injunction to a large crowd which hooted and jeered. Several newspaper reporters who were present claimed that this crowd was made up not of railroad men, but of young men from the town and brickyard workers, as in previous disturbances. It was ARU men, in fact, who urged the crowd to disperse.

VI Property Damage versus Human Lives

There are exact figures in the USSC report on the

amount of property damage done during the strike, but there are no official figures on the number of people shot and wounded by the police, national guardsmen, federal troops, federal marshals, and railway detectives. Nowhere in the hearings did any member of the commission inquire how many people were killed or injured, or exactly who was responsible for these shootings. But there was, by contrast, intensive questioning as to the amount of property damage and the persons responsible for it. Ray Ginger claims that thirty persons were killed and twice as many injured during the "riots," with thirteen of them killed and 53 seriously injured in the city of Chicago.

The first death apparently occurred on the night of July 5. In Kensington, just west of Pullman, one man, a mere spectator to disorder there, was killed after having been shot twice by a man named Stark, variously described as a U.S. deputy marshal (Carwardine, herein, p. 39) and a railway detective (USSC, pp. 369, 505). He could have been both. Two were also wounded in that incident. On the night of July 7, as already indicated, a woman was killed by police on the northwest side, and three more, at least, were killed by police or militia at 49th and Loomis, two blocks from the Stockyards. The same night an innocent man, searching for his lost son, was killed when U.S. troops fired into a crowd in the railway yards at Hammond, Ind., just across the state line. At Spring Valley, 90 miles southwest of Chicago, on July 10, a special train carrying a detachment of U.S. troops and deputy marshals was stoned by coal miners. Soldiers fired upon them, killing two and wounding eight.

The above eight deaths are the only ones mentioned in the strike commission report. There is no information that any person was ever indicted for any of these shootings, or even that an inquest or grand jury hearing was held on any of them. The USSC likewise showed no concern about them. So much for commentary on the value placed on human life by all the machinery of government at that time. No one on the company's side was killed. Had there been, would there have been the same lack of concern?

According to the commission report, "The mobs ...were, by general concurrence in testimony, composed of hoodlums, women, a low class of foreigners, and recruits from the criminal classes." (USSC, xlvi). Moreover, according to testimony of a newspaper reporter, a crowd overturning cars at 27th street and the Rock Island tracks were mostly blacks. Or, as might have been reported in another place at another time, they were just "gooks."

The amount of property damage caused by the strike, including burned cars and losses of perishable goods, was placed at less than $700,000. The chief economic cost of the strike was clearly in the lost earnings of workers and corporations and the expenses of police and military intervention.

The scene of perhaps the most mob action during the strike-boycott was in the vicinity of the Rock Island yard and shops at 51st and State Streets. The tracks at this point were shared by several railroads terminating at the LaSalle street station and trains were frequently blocked by overturned cars. On the nights of July 4, 5, and 6, cars were set afire here and elsewhere largely by bands of youths. On the night of July 6 crowds looted and set fire to hundreds of cars in the Panhandle yards on the southwest side. Seven cars were burned at Blue Island, and the fire department was called, but, according to Everett St. John of the GMA, when it was found that the fire was on railroad property, they returned to their quarters without attempting to extinguish the fires.

Similar eruptions took place elsewhere, and on the single night of July 6, according to Lindsey, damage totalled $340,000, or half the total losses during the entire strike.

There is evidence that some of these fires were the work of paid agents of the GMA to turn public sentiment against the strike, and some were set by temporary U.S. marshals to justify their continued employment. (Lindsey, pp. 216-17).

On the afternoon of the 7th occurred the worst bloodshed, when a crowd of people trying to block the movement of a wrecking train just south of the Stockyards was charged with bayonets by the militia, and then fired upon by police and militia. Accounts vary, but three or four were killed and a score were wounded. (See pp *xxi*, *xxvii*)

VII Court Action and Defeat

A special grand jury was called together on July 10th by district attorney Thomas Milchrist and special counsel Edwin Walker, to consider charges against ARU officers of conspiracy to interfere with the movement of mail. Copies of telegrams, subpoenaed from Western Union, were the only evidence introduced. After two hours, the jurors indicted Eugene Debs, vice-president George W. Howard, secretary Sylvester Keliher, and editor Lewis W. Rogers of the *Railway Times*. All were arrested that day, and after a few hours detention, were released on bail of $10,000 each. Meanwhile a squad of deputy marshals and postal inspectors ransacked the union headquarters, and confiscated books, papers, and correspondence, including the unopened personal mail of Eugene Debs. District attorney Milchrist was later corrected for this excess of zeal by Judge Grosscup, and Debs' papers were ordered returned to him.

On July 17 Debs and his fellow officers were again arrested and charged with contempt of court for violation of the injunction of July 2. A hearing on the charges was set for July 23, and bail was placed at $3,000 each. This time Debs and his fellow officers rejected bail and remained in jail until the hearing. At the hearing the defense demanded, and was denied, a jury trial. When Edwin Walker became ill, the hearing was continued until September 5, and bail was increased to $10,000. Debs and his fellows decided to make bail.

The legal harassment of the union leadership seriously hampered the conduct of the strike. Communications with local leaders around the country was blocked, and morale began to wither. A few trains began to move on July 10, and by July 13, in Lindsey's estimate, the strikers in Chicago had been virtually beaten. On July 8 a meeting representing a hundred Chicago unions told Pullman he must negotiate by the 10th or they would call a general strike. But by the 10th the ARU leaders were in jail or on bond, troops were in command of the city and only about 25,000 workers walked out, with no major effect.

On July 12 Samuel Gompers and the AFL executive council met at Chicago in response to demands that it come to the aid of the beleaguered rail workers. Since the ARU was not an AFL affiliate and was in fact an industrial union, an organizational rival of the shop crafts repairing trains and affiliated with the AFL, and a rival also of the operating Brotherhoods that the AFL hoped might affiliate, and especially since the plan of organization of the ARU was one with which the AFL leadership was at war, no helpful action could be expected. Ever cautious and conservative, the AFL leaders limited themselves to asking President Cleveland to "lend your influence and give us your aid so that the present industrial crisis may be brought to an end," and to come to Chicago or send a deputy. The president did not answer. Debs addressed the AFL leaders but did not ask anything from them. If words could be of any help, Gompers next day issued a public statement of sympathy for the strikers, and denounced Pullman:

> In this strike of the American Railway Union we recognize an impulsive vigorous protest against the gathering, growing forces of plutocratic power and corporation rule. In the sympathetic movement of that order to help the Pullman employees, they have demonstrated the hollow shams of Pullman's

pharisaical paradise. Mr. Pullman in his persistent repulses of arbitration and in his heartless autocratic treatment of his employees has proven himself a public enemy.

Against this array of armed force and brutal moneyed aristocracy would it not be worse than folly to call men out on a general or local strike in these days of stagnant trade and commercial depression?

No; better let us organize more generally, combine more closely, unite our forces, educate and prepare ourselves to protect our interests, and that we may go to the ballot box and cast our votes as American freemen united and determined to redeem this country from its present political industrial misrule, to take it from the hands of the plutocratic wreckers and place it in the hands of the common people. (USSC, p. 193).

As Mr. Gompers later told the strike commission, the AFL leaders believed "it would be most unwise, as well as inexpedient, as well as detrimental to the interests of labor, to call a general strike in sympathy with the American Railway Union or the Pullman strikers." (USSC, p. 191). Therefore, "with the adoption of that report, an expression of good will and a resolution recommending to the executive council proper the appropriation of $1,000 toward the defense fund for Mr. Debs, the conference adjourned."

There were of course numerous dramatic actions elsewhere, particularly in New Mexico, Colorado, and California, in each of which federal and state troops were called out. At Raton, New Mexico, railroad men were compelled to work at the point of a bayonet. The governors of these states, like Altgeld, protested without effect against federal interference.

VIII After the Strike

On July 18 the Pullman management posted the following notice on the plant gates: "These shops will be opened as soon as the number of operatives taken on is sufficient to make a working force in all departments." The next day, the first withdrawal of state and federal troops began, and the last militia departed from Chicago on August 7.

Applications for employment at Pullman continued until by August 24 the rolls included 2,337 men, of whom 1778 were "former employees," and 599 were new. The repair department opened on August 2, and other departments opened as the work force grew. Every striker rehired was required to surrender his union card and sign a yellow dog contract pledging not to join any union while working for Pullman. (The company officials claimed before the USSC that they had no objection to unions in general).

One worker, Theodore Rhodie, a painter, was among those who did not try to regain their jobs at Pullman. When asked the reason by Mr. Worthington of the USSC, he replied:

There is one reason, and that is, I do not like to walk up there and hand up my membership in the American Railway Union because when a man asks me to give up my principles, my rights as an American citizen, he might just as well ask for my life.

Strikers not rehired were blacklisted by Pullman and by all railroads. Many would get a job elsewhere, only to be fired as soon as their former employers replied to inquiries from the new ones. Many changed their names and falsified their work history in order to get around the blacklist, an option which was still possible before Social Security and Railroad Retirement made the system harder to beat. Many who were unable to get around the blacklist were relentlessly pursued without pity from job to job and forced into complete destitution. The challenged Master was harsh and unforgiving, determined to teach the errant workers a lesson they would not forget.

Though the Pullman strike was a defeat which

wrecked the American Railway Union beyond repair, and banished unionism from the Pullman works for decades, it was not a total loss. Thousands of workers were educated by it, workers are still inspired by it, and many employers learned that victory for them could be as costly as defeat for the workers. Pullman's losses during the three month shutdown far exceeded what it would have cost to yield to the modest demands of the workers. As for George M. Pullman, who had some concern for his place in history, he was destined to be regarded as a stubborn, ungenerous, autocrat and a prime example of all that was worst about capitalism in his time. The Cleveland industrialist Mark Hanna commented that any employer who refused to talk with with his men was a damned fool. (Buder, p. 200). Sam Gompers called him "the most consummate type of avaricious wealth absorber, tyrant, and hypocrite this age...has furnished." Carwardine held that "he has reaped the censure and universal condemnation of the press and public opinion of the country."

Pullman died a hated man in October, 1897, and was buried under tons of steel and concrete, topped by a Corinthian column, in Chicago's Graceland cemetery, where Altgeld would also rest four years later. History has been much kinder to Pullman's opponents, Altgeld, Debs, and Darrow, than to him. His feudal town was dissolved by order of the Supreme Court of Illinois a decade after his death, the company being required to divest itself of all properties not needed for manufacturing purposes, as such a company town was "incompatible with the theory and spirit of our institutions."

On the 15th of August, 1894, the United States Strike Commission appointed by President Cleveland began its hearings in Chicago. Its members were Carroll D. Wright, U.S. commissioner of labor, chairman, and two lawyers, John D. Kernan of New York and Nicholas Worthington of Peoria, Ill. In thirteen days of hearings at Chicago, the commission heard 107 witnesses, and at another session in Washington on September 26, heard two more witnesses. Included among them were all of the important figures in the strike, union and company officers, public officials, railroad workers and managers, police, marshals, militia officers, strikers, and news reporters. The commission produced a 681 page volume of testimony, preceded by a 34 page report. Despite the conservative composition of the commission, its report was on the whole supportive of the union and critical of the Pullman Company and the General Managers Association. It declared that "The Pullman Company is hostile to the idea of conferring with organized labor in the settlement of differences arising between it and its employees." The General Managers Association was deemed "an illustration of the persistent and shrewdly devised plans of corporations to overreach their limitations and to usurp indirectly powers and rights not contemplated in their charters and not obtainable from the people or their legislators." It pointed out that "until the railroads set the example, a general union of railroad employees was never attempted." It found the union economic contentions substantially correct: through wage cuts and high rents the company was shifting the whole burden of the depression to its workers with no sacrifice to its profits. It found labor ready to negotiate but the company and General Managers Association completely unwilling, the latter actively co-ordinating resistance to the strike and recruiting strikebreakers.

With regard to the injunction of July 2, for alleged violation of which the ARU leaders were arrested, the commission said it "seriously questioned and with much force, whether courts have jurisdiction to enjoin citizens from 'persuading' each other in industrial or other matters of common interest.

Violence during the strike was blamed on "shiftless adventurers and criminals" and mobs which contained "many of a certain class of objectionable foreigners, who are being precipitated upon us by unrestricted immigration." There was "no evidence before the commission that the officers of the American Railway

Union at any time participated in or advised intimidation, violence, or destruction of property." The ultimate blame for the trouble was placed on society: "Many impartial observers are reaching the view that much of the real responsibility for these disorders rests with the people themselves and with the Government for not adequately controlling monopolies and corporations, and for failing to reasonably protect the rights of labor and redress its wrongs."

Concerning the U.S. marshals the commission declared:

They were armed and paid by the railroads, and acted in the double capacity of railroad employees and United States officers. While operating the railroads they assumed and exercised unrestricted United States authority when so ordered by their employers, or whenever they regarded it as necessary. They were not under the direct control of any Government official while exercising authority. This is placing officers of the government under control of a combination of railroads. It is a bad precedent, which might well lead to serious consequences.

The commission's solution to the problems revealed by the strike was a series of proposed reforms which were, in part, embodied in the National Railway Labor Act passed 32 years later. "Since nations have grown to the wisdom of deciding disputes by conciliation, and even of settling them by arbitration," they argued, "Why should capital and labor in their dependence upon each other persist in cutting each others throats as a settlement of differences?"

The commission urged that unions were preferable, as England had found, to the chaos that preceded them, and complained that "some of the courts, however, are still poring over the law reports of antiquity in order to construe conspiracy out of labor unions." Moreover, in view of the "progressive perversion of the law of supply and demand by capital and changed conditions, no man can deny the right nor dispute the wisdom of unity for legislative and protective purposes among those who supply labor.''

The commission endorsed the establishment of a permanent government commission for fact finding and conciliation or arbitration, but shrank from endorsement of public ownership of railroads, while yet entertaining the idea as a possible future necessity: "Should continued combinations and consolidations result in half a dozen or less ownerships of our railroads within a few years, as is by no means unlikely, the question of Government ownership will be forced to the front, and we need to be ready to dispose of it intelligently. As combination goes on there will certainly at least have to be greater Government regulation and control of quasi-public corporations than we have now.'' (Eugene Debs drew applause when he told the commission that "Government ownership of railroads is decidedly better for the people than railroad ownership of Government.'' For workers and socialists, of course, the question is, "Whose government?'')

The permanent commission recommended by USSC would have the power of the Interstate Commerce Commission to compel railroads to obey its decisions, after hearings. Companies and unions could each appoint a temporary member of the commission during the pendency of controversies affecting them, but the unions would be required to incorporate in order to be so recognized. Companies, during pendency of proceedings inaugurated by a union could not discharge employees except for specified causes, and unions could not call strikes during the same period. Yellow dog contracts, requiring men to agree not to join unions, or to leave them if already a member, as a condition of employment, should be outlawed, the commission said. Employers were urged to recognize unions, and were advised that "while the interests of labor and capital are not identical, they are reciprocal.''

The commission report was vigorously denounced in *Harper's Weekly* (November 24, 1894) which warned that "If the mass of our citizens think as this commission thinks, this first stage in a socialistic revolution is already far advanced, and the transformation of our nineteenth century civilization into something widely different, and as yet wholly unimagined, is a process which cannot long be delayed." The commission was charged with a "labored and persistent effort" to "relieve from reproach the strikers, rioters and friends of disorder, and to exhibit as unwise or questionable every principal step to oppose them."

Grover Cleveland ignored the report, making no reference to it in his Princeton address previously mentioned, but Eugene Debs quoted it with approval, in his answer to Cleveland which was published in the *Appeal to Reason*, August 27, 1904, after being rejected by *McClure's* magazine. Cleveland's own commission, wrote Debs, "charges him, in effect, with serving the railroads as a strike-breaker by furnishing government employees to take the places of striking railroad men and arming them with pistols and clubs and with all the authority of government officials."

"Hundreds of pages of evidence," Debs charged, "are given by impartial witnesses to establish the guilt of the railroad corporations, to prove that the leaders of the strike counseled peace and order; that the strikers themselves were law abiding and used their influence to prevent disorder; that there was no trouble until the murderous deputy marshals were sprung upon the community."

IX Trials and Jail

The last postscript to the Pullman strike is the trial and imprisonment of Eugene Debs and his fellow union leaders, George W. Howard, L. W. Rogers, Sylvester Keliher, William E. Burns, Ray Goodwin, Martin J. Elliott, and James Hogan. The last four had been arrested August 1st and charged with contempt, following the preliminary hearing of the others who were previously arrested. All faced the court on September 5, Judge William A. Woods presiding. The defense consisted of E. E. Erwin, S. S. Gregory, and Clarence Darrow, the last named on leave from service as a lawyer for the Northwestern Railway. The defendants did not choose to testify and no witnesses were called on their behalf to answer a string of prosecution witnesses. Instead, in hearings that lasted most of the month, the defense confined itself to legal arguments that the court had no authority under the Sherman Act to issue the injunction of July 2; that the defendants had not interfered with movement of mail or interstate commerce, and had never urged lawless acts; and that the denial of trial by jury and the punishment of the accused for both conspiracy and contempt, for the same alleged offense, constituted double jeopardy, illegal under the constitution.

The judge dallied until December 14 before handing down his decision, in order that he might write a document fit for the ages, filled with learned citations. He upheld the government entirely, and sentenced Debs to six months imprisonment and his co-defendants to three months. They were to serve their time in the McHenry County jail at Woodstock, fifty miles from Chicago, and it was here that they appeared on January 8, 1895, to pay the debt that uncorrupted men must often pay for challenging ruthless power.

On January 24 the trial for conspiracy began at Chicago, for which purpose the defendants had to be transported from and to Woodstock each day. Mr. Pullman himself left town, as he also had early in the strike, to avoid subpoena. After the trial was over, Pullman, flanked by his attorney and first vice-president, Robert Todd Lincoln, son of the Emancipator, would meet in chambers with Judge Grosscup.

The conspiracy charge was so transparently contrived that the jurors were, according to Darrow's later remarks, 11 to 1 for acquittal. However, they never had an opportunity to vote one way or another, for, when one juror took sick on February 8, the judge dismissed the entire jury, bringing the trial to an end. It was never resumed.

Meanwhile an appeal against the contempt sentence had been carried to the Supreme Court by a defense team consisting of S. S. Gregory, Clarence Darrow, and the 81 year old Lyman Trumbull, former senator, Lincoln supporter, and author of the thirteenth amendment. Oral arguments were heard March 26-27, on the petition for a writ of habeas corpus, and two months later the petition was denied in a unanimous decision by Justice Brewer. The Republic was safe.

The defense had argued, as in the Chicago trial, that the Sherman act of 1890 should not be used in a labor dispute, as this was contrary to the intent of the legislators at the time of its enactment, and that the defendants had never urged a single unlawful act. It was again argued that they had been illegally denied a jury trial. All the arguments were unavailing, and the defendants served out their time, while the union died.

In Woodstock Debs received letters and pamphlets from Socialists and was visited by Victor Berger, Socialist publisher from Milwaukee. Berger brought with him books by Marx and Kautsky. Debs was ready for their message. He had grown tired of politics after a term in the Indiana legislature. In July during his last strike address he had declared, "I am a Populist and I favor wiping out both old parties...I have been a Democrat all my life and I am ashamed to admit it...Go to the polls and vote the People's ticket." In August he had explained his views to the commission:

Comr. Wright: Do you believe there is no solution of any of these problems under the present industrial system? Ans.: No sir; that is my candid conviction.

Comr. Kernan: Then government ownership of railroads is only an expedient; it is not a final solution after all? Ans.: It could be a final solution so far as the railroads are concerned, but not of other matters.

Comr. Kernan: Then would government ownership

of all trades and property follow as a solution of the other? Ans.: I believe in a cooperative commonwealth as a substitute for the wage system. Comr. Wright: Another name for state socialism? Ans.: No, sir; I do not call myself a socialist. There is a wide difference in the interpretation or definition of the term. I believe in a co-operative commonwealth upon the principles laid down by Laurence Gronlund....In relation to the wage system, in my judgment—I am studying this question and want much more light than I have got—I am impressed with the conviction that social and industrial conditions will grow worse...If a man is obliged to depend on another man as to whether he shall work or not, he is a slave. (USSC 169-170)

In 1897 Debs and the shreds of the ARU organized the Social Democracy of America, a part of which became the Social Democratic Party the next year. This group, in cooperation with a splinter from the Socialist Labor Party, ran Debs as Socialist candidate for President in 1900, and he joined in the Unity Convention which created the Socialist Party at Indianapolis in 1901. Debs was also a participant in the founding convention of the Industrial Workers of the World in 1905. He became, to masses of Americans, Mr. Socialist, until his death at Elmhurst, Ill., on October 20, 1926. It seems apparent that the last thirty years of his career were strongly influenced by the lessons of the Pullman strike.

X Conclusions

What is the historical importance of the Pullman strike? It was not a mere passing ripple on the waves of history. Many a cause that seems lost at one time is merely a cause not yet won. First the strike laid bare certain features of the American system. It illustrated the close harmony between the courts, the federal government, and the corporations in dealing with labor, in that period at least. It revealed clearly the myth of the government as a neutral and impartial arbiter in class struggles. It proved the inadequacy of a divided, craft-ridden labor movement in dealing with the united power of big business and government. It indicated that the economic power of labor could be frustrated by the political power of capital, and taught that labor must seek political power to buttress its industrial strength.

Even a lost strike, Gompers told the strike commission, is a "warning to the employing class generally that the workingmen will not go down further, that any attempt to force them down will be very expensive." A discharged Rock Island yardmaster felt that the eventual unification of labor was foreshadowed. George P. Lovejoy held that "The strike we have just passed through will be a benefit to the laboring men of the country for years to come. It will demonstrate to the laboring men that they must get together, that no single organization can win."

There are other gains that the Pullman strike may have promoted. It discredited the paternalistic company town idea and perhaps halted its spread. By its influence on Debs and others this strike influenced the development both of American socialism and industrial unionism. It was a part of the long slow process by which some of the worst excesses against workers were effectively fought where they were not abolished: certain types of injunction, the blacklist, the labor spy system and yellow dog contracts.

Finally, the Pullman strike furnished an example of solidarity, of nobility and heroism, by both leaders and rank and file, which inspired generations of fighters for human liberation here and abroad. It was a glowing light to prove that in a world governed largely by acquisitiveness and rapacity, there were still enough people responding to a different drummer, to give promise that freedom for the oppressed was not a utopian dream but a practical goal.

REV. WILLIAM H. CARWARDINE, 1863-1929

by William Adelman

Rev. William H. Carwardine, minister of the first Methodist church of Pullman, more than any other man awakened the American public to the suffering of the people of Pullman. His book, *The Pullman Strike*, his many speeches throughout the city of Chicago, and his address before the American Railway Union convention helped to gain both labor and public support for the citizens of Pullman.

Rev. Carwardine was a Populist, a friend of labor, and an early advocate of the "social gospel." Enemies accused him of being an anarchist. Although he was at first condemned by this church, in September of 1894 the Methodist Church in Chicago gave him support.

Carwardine was active in the Pullman Relief Committee, which gathered food, clothing and money for the strikers, and he also became the director of the Homeseekers' Association, an organization established after the strike to find new jobs and homes for the thousands of strikers that were blacklisted. Carwardine was so successful in getting new jobs in Chicago and throughout the country for the blacklisted strikers that his own congregation dropped from 300 to only 100 members, and he was transferred to the Methodist church in Packingtown, the area around the Chicago Stockyards. As the minister of this church, he showed the same concern for his congregation as he had shown in Pullman.

Later he lectured in 64 cities throughout the country under the auspices of trade and labor organizations, Chautauquas, and private clubs. He spoke on "The Industrial Problem in America." The following are typical statements he made during his tour:

"The rights of property are now warring on the rights of man."

"If there is one law for the rich man and another for the poor man, there is no liberty."

"Christ came to turn things upside down."

As an advocate of "ballots instead of bullets" as a way of changing society, Rev. Carwardine ran for the Illinois State Senate from the 27th district in 1904 on the Prohibition ticket. He was personally endorsed by Samuel Gompers. Although he lost the election, the following year he became the religious editor of the Chicago *Herald-Examiner,* a position he held until his death.

Rev. Carwardine was a great American, who believed that the society of his day had distorted government to serve big business' vested interests. He did not wish to destroy American capitalism but wished to put capitalism behind the Constitution where it belonged, instead of ahead of the Constitution, where it was in practice.

He died in Evanston, Illinois, on Sunday, August 25, 1929, and was buried in Memorial Park cemetery in that city.

ANNOTATED BIBLIOGRAPHY
By Virgil J. Vogel

Addams, Jane. "A Modern Lear," in Ray Ginger, *American Social Thought*. New York: Hill & Wang, 1969. A hard look at George Pullman's paternalism and arrogance.

Adelman, William. *Touring Pullman*: A Study in Company Paternalism; a Walking Guide to the Pullman Community in Chicago, Illinois. Chicago: Illinois Labor History Society, 1972. All the important historical sites of Pullman are here illustrated and their history described.

Ashley, W. J. *The Railroad Strike of 1894*. The Statement of the Pullman Company and the Report of the Commission, together with an Analysis of the Issues. Cambridge: The Church Social Union, 1895. Documents only, little analysis.

Bancroft, Edgar A. *The Chicago Strike of 1894*. Chicago: privately printed, 1895. A lawyer's brief for the Pullman company, completely biased against the union.

Barnard, Harry. *Eagle Forgotten*: the Life of John Peter Altgeld. Indianapolis: Charter Books, 1962. Narrates the progressive governor's conflict with President Cleveland over troops in the Pullman strike.

Brecher, Jeremy. *Strike!* San Francisco: Straight Arrow Press, 1972. An illustrated description and analysis of major strikes 1877 to 1946; gives extensive account of Pullman episodes in west.

Buder, Stanley. *Pullman:* an Experiment in Industrial Order and Community Planning, 1880-1930. New York: Oxford University Press, 1967. The focus is on the history of the company and the Pullman community; too uncritical of Mr. Pullman in places, and prone to accept his claims at face value.

Carwardine, Rev. William H. *The Pullman Strike.* Chicago: Charles H. Kerr Co., 1894. Reprint for the Illinois Labor History Society, 1971. New edition, with new introduction, 1973.

Cleveland, Grover. *The Government in the Chicago Strike of 1894.* Princeton: Princeton University Press, 1913. A lecture given at Princeton University in 1904, self serving and one-sided. It was published in *McClure's* magazine for July, 1904, which refused to accept a reply from Debs. For his reply, published in the *Appeal to Reason,* see below, under Debs.

Coleman, McAlister. *Eugene V. Debs, A Man Unafraid.* New York: Greenberg, 1930. The first biography of Debs, by a Socialist comrade, written with a warmth missing in academic accounts.

Debs, Eugene. *Debs: His Life, Writings and Speeches.* St. Louis: Phil Wagner, 1908. Contains "The Federal Government and the Chicago Strike," Debs' reply to Cleveland's 1904 Princeton lecture on the Pullman strike. "How I Became a Socialist" relates his experience in Woodstock jail.

Debs, Eugene. *Writings and Speeches of Eugene V. Debs.* New York: Hermitage Press, Inc. Contains several articles relating to the Pullman strike and railroad workers; the book is marred by an insipid introduction by Arthur M. Schlesinger, Jr.

Ginger, Ray. *The Bending Cross:* A Biography of Eugene Victor Debs. New Brunswick, N.J.: Rutgers University Press, 1949. Part II, "The American Railway Union," almost 100 pages long, has excellent review of the strike.

Karsner, David. *Debs, His Authorized Life and Letters.* New York: Boni and Livewright, 1919. See chapter VII, "Labor Unionist and Woodstock." Has many direct Debs quotes.

Lens, Sidney. *The Labor Wars.* From Molly Maguires to the Sitdowns. Garden City, N.Y.: Doubleday, 1973. Has a well researched chapter on the Pullman strike, "The Debs Revolution."

Lindsey, Almont. *The Pullman Strike.* The Story of a Unique Experiment and of a Great Labor Upheaval. Chicago: University of Chicago Press, 1942, 1964. The standard, scholarly study, well documented.

Nimmo, Joseph Jr. *The Insurrection of June and July, 1894.* Washington, D.C.: Age Printing Co., 1894. Legalistic address, drained of all human juices, biased in favor of Cleveland.

Painter, Floy Ruth. *That Man Debs and His Life Work.* Bloomington, Ind.: Graduate Council, Indiana University, 1929. Pp. 14-75 deals with the ARU, Pullman strike, and Woodstock jail. Pp. 18-72 deals with the strike and its results. Academic, but sympathetic to Debs.

Radosh, Ronald. *Debs.* Englewood Cliffs, N.J.: Prentice-Hall, 1971. Anthology of documents, the first of which is Debs' proclamation to the ARU, written from jail, June 1, 1895, after the Supreme Court turned down his appeal.

Shannon, David A. *The Socialist Party of America.* New York: MacMillan, 1955. A general account of the movement with which Debs was identified after the Pullman strike.

Stead, W. T. *Chicago To-Day, or the Labour War in America.* London: Review of Reveiws, 1894. Observations of the town of Pullman and the strike, while it was still on, by a British observer; sympathetic to the union.

United States Strike Commission. *Report of the Chicago Strike of June-July, 1894.* Washington: Government Printing Office, 1895. Contains lengthy testimony by Eugene Debs, George Pullman, William Carwardine, Thomas H. Wickes, and many other persons connected with the strike. It has been extensively used in preparing the introduction for this edition of *The Pullman Strike.*

United States Supreme Court. *Ex Parte in the Matter of Eugene V. Debs et al.* October, 1894. Contains all of the legal briefs of both sides in connection with the conviction of Debs and other union officers for violation of the injunction issued at Chicago on July 2, 1894, and the court's decision.

Warne, Colston E., ed. *The Pullman Boycott of 1894.* The Problem of Federal Intervention. Lexington, Mass : D. C. Heath, 1955. Contains the text of several documents and articles relating to the strike, the best easily available collection.

AFFECTIONATELY DEDICATED

TO MY

BELOVED FATHER-IN-LAW

REV. JOHN WILLIAMS

PASTOR OF THE FIRST M. E. CHURCH, CRESTON, ILL.

WHO WAS

FOR THIRTY YEARS IN HIS EARLY LIFE CONNECTED WITH THE
DAILY PRESS OF NEW YORK CITY, AND WHO DID
LOYAL SERVICE AT THAT TIME IN AROUS-
ING PUBLIC SENTIMENT TO THE
NEEDS OF THE TOIL-
ING MASSES

CONTENTS.

———

Coming from the Relief Store.

INTRODUCTION.

This book is packed with facts. For these facts the author is not responsible. It is true, his soul was stirred, but cruel facts stirred the soul of even the Son of God. If sometimes the author's spirit flames with indignation, let it be remembered that it is against heartless tyranny, and in defense of long silent and outraged innocence.

He speaks with authority. He is a resident of Pullman, and is familiar with almost every face and fireside in the town. Like his Master, he has gone about doing good, among the rich and poor alike. He knows Pullman and his lieutenants. He knows Debs and his most trusted followers. He knows what both sides have done, when, and how, and why, and with what results. In a sense, therefore, he knows more about the whole conflict than either Debs or Pullman. Each knows his own side only. The author of this volume knows both sides.

The book is reliable. The author means to neither minify nor magnify. He would be a mere photographer. Assuredly he has not fallen into the error of exaggeration. No student, lecturer, preacher or reformer need hesitate in using the statements herein made. They can all be verified again and again.

With all my heart, I bid this book God-speed! May it be read in a million of homes, from the White House to the dug-out, and from the palaces of millionaires down to the hovels of the humble poor. May its plain, honest facts banish the flagrant misinformation with which the secular and even the religious press has been teeming for weeks, and may it be the mission of this book to stir the heart of this whole nation until the "white slaves" of industrial tyranny be emancipated and receive the treatment becoming the sons and daughters of the Most High.

JOHN MERRITTE DRIVER.

Marion, Ind., July 30th, 1894

The Strikers' Relief Headquarters at Kensington.

THE PULLMAN STRIKE.

CHAPTER I.

INTRODUCTORY.

The Pullman strike is the greatest and most far-reaching of any strike on record in this country. It is the most unique strike ever known. When we take into account the intelligence of the employees, always the boast of the Pullman Company; the widespread advertisement of the town as a "model town," established as a solution of the industrial problem upon the basis of "mutual recognition;" it is no wonder that the world was amazed, when, under such apparently favorable conditions, in the midst of a season of great financial depression, the employees laid down their tools, and, on the 11th of May, walked out of the great shops to face an unequal and apparently hopeless conflict.

After seven weeks of patient waiting, the American Railway Union, having espoused the cause of the Pullman employees, declares a boycott on the Pullman Palace Cars. This action is repulsed by the

Railroad Managers' Association. The conflict is transferred at once to the arena of public commerce; organized labor and organized capital are pitted against each other; stagnation of all business interests results; the highways of trade are blocked; the great unoffending public is the innocent sufferer, riots ensue, the military are ordered out, the foundations of government are threatened; the strong arm of the law is put forth, the public demand for peace is heard, and the crisis reached.

Now the public mind reverts to the original cause. What made these intelligent employees at Pullman strike? Were they rash and inconsiderate, or were they driven to their course by certain conditions over which they had no control, and which justified them in their action?

These and a hundred other questions are coming to me by every mail from all parts of our country. Ten days after the employees struck, I delivered a sermon from my pulpit, which created profound interest in Pullman and Chicago, and which has since been copied broadcast in newspapers all over the United States. Owing to this fact, I am accosted on all sides for information concerning the true condition of things in this model town.

For two years I have been the pastor of the Pullman M. E. Church, and closely related to the moral and social life of the town. During that time I have been a silent spectator of the life and character of the town. I have studied carefully and with much interest the Pullman system. I have had abundant opportunity to observe the town from the standpoint of a student of the industrial problem.

I wish to be fair and impartial. I have seen many things to admire as well as many to condemn. My sympathies have gone out to the striking employees. Never did men have a cause more just—never did corporation with equal pretenses grind men more unmercifully. I contend that I have a right to publicly criticise a public man or a public institution, so long as I do not depart from the path of truth or make false imputations, willfully knowing them to be such. No one has deplored this strike more than myself. I wish that it might have been averted. But so long as the employees saw fit to take this action I believe that it is the duty of all concerned to look the issue squarely in the face, without equivocation or evasion, consider the matter in its true light, and endeavor to bring about a settlement of the difficulty as speedily as possible.

I make no apology as a clergyman for discussing this theme. As ministers of the gospel we have a right to occasionally turn from the beaten path of biblical truth and consider these great questions of social, moral and economic interest. He who denies the right of the clergy to discuss these matters of great public concern has either been brought up under a government totally foreign to the free atmosphere of

American institutions, or else he has failed utterly to comprehend the spirit of the age in which he lives.

Sometimes we preachers are told to mind our own business and "preach the gospel." All right; I have preached the gospel of Christ, and souls have been redeemed to a better life under the preaching of that gospel. ´ I contend now that in the discussing of this theme I am preaching the gospel of applied Christianity—applied to humanity—the gospel of mutual recognition, of co-operation, of the "brotherhood of humanity." The relation existing between a man's body and his soul are such that you can make very little headway appealing to the soul of a thoroughly live and healthy man if he be starving for food. Christ not only preached to the multitude, but he gave them to eat. And I verily believe that if he came to Chicago to-day, as indicated by the erratic yet noble Stead, he would apply the whip of cords to the backs of some of us preachers for not performing our full share of duty to "his poor."

> "Let not ambition mock their useful toil,
> Their homely joys, and destiny obscure;
> Nor grandeur hear with a disdainful smile
> The short and simple annals of the poor."

CHAPTER II.

THE TOWN OF PULLMAN.

"The Pullman car solved the problem of long, continuous railway journeys, and the town of Pullman, along new lines, gives a hope of bettering the relations of capital and labor. The issue of this last is a question of the future, but it is at least a legitimate subject of speculation, whether what the car wrought in one direction, with all its attendant and lasting benefits to humanity, may not in some sort, on a broader scale, and with benefits to humanity even more far-reaching and enduring, be repeated in the great field where the town of Pullman now stands as the advance guard of a new departure and a new idea.

"In brief, the Pullman enterprise is a vast object-lesson. It has demonstrated man's capacity to improve and to appreciate improvements. It has shown that success may result from corporate action which is alike free from default, foreclosure or wreckage of any sort. It has illustrated the helpful combination of capital and labor, without strife or stultification, upon lines of mutual recognition."

The above is taken from a work entitled "The Story of Pullman," referred to in another place and written in the interest of Pullman. In view of the above it may be well to say a few words concerning the town of Pullman itself. The story as told in

15

1894 is a far different one.   There is strife, mutual
suspicion and discord.   There are strikes, lockouts
and the inevitable violence, riots, arson and murder
resulting therefrom, which certainly indicates that
there must be something wrong in Pullman.   I believe that the town itself was established in the hope
of bettering the condition of the laboring classes, but
it has failed sadly of its original purpose.   As seen
from the railway by the passing tourist, it presents a
beautiful picture.   In fact it appears to be a veritable
paradise.   Beautiful trees and flowers, pretty foun-
tains, glimpses here and there of artistic sweeps of
landscape, gardens, rows of pretty little brick houses,
church in the distance, public buildings of different
description, all present a beautiful picture to the
passing traveler.

Mr. Pullman and his lieutenants love to show this
beautiful picture to the world.   Pullman, the town,
is Mr. Pullman's idol, and in many respects he may
well be proud of it, but there is another side to the
town of Pullman.   Like the stage, there is something behind the scenes, and that which is behind the
scenes does not harmonize with the effect produced
before the curtain.   Let us take a short tour around
the town.   We will enter the Arcade.   In this building is the postoffice, stores of different descriptions,
the Opera House, offices of the town agent and his
clerical force, and on the second story, library and
rooms of the Young Men's Christian Association and

Kindergarten. Also one or two rooms devoted to the use of churches, one room of which the Baptist church occupied up to within a few weeks ago, when under the active administration of the noble pastor, Rev. Fred Berry, they have succeeded in building a church on the outskirts of Pullman, in Roseland. Another room is rented by the Episcopal church.

Note for a few moments the library. It is a gem. It is one of the most complete of its kind in the United States. It is small and cozy, but very convenient for those who have the privilege of using it. It was the gift of Mr. Pullman to his town. The library is presided over by Mrs. Charles B. Smith, librarian, a lady who is intimately related to Mr. Pullman, entirely in sympathy with all his ideas and one who is regarded with the highest estimation by the people of the entire town. As president of the Woman's Relief Society, she, together with other ladies, has endeared herself to the poor and the suffering in Pullman. The library rooms are luxurious and are regarded by all visitors as the handsomest in this country. It has 8,000 volumes, covering every practical department of knowledge. The whole number of books used in 1893 was 20,900. I note in an enumerated table, the number taken from each department, as printed in the Pullman Journal of last year. Of reference books there were used 5,479; of books for juveniles, 2,343; books of fiction, 3,161. History, 1,406; biography, 1,057; of science, 2,245;

travels, 1,245, and of poetry 2,073. Judging from
the last, it is evident that the artistic effect and influence of Pullman upon the inhabitants causes them to
indulge in much poetry.

While we admire the library and believe that it is
doing good work, still it is not producing the practical
results demanded of such an institution. The complaint of employees is that they are expected to pay
25 cents a month or three dollars a year for the use
of books, and one dollar per year for every child.
This is all right, but with the immense wealth
of the Pullman Company they feel that they ought to
have an absolutely free library and reading room.
The reading room is an adjunct of the library, is very
small, and very few of the men, comparatively speak-
ing, use it. It is too luxurious for the average working man. It has a tendency to create a spirit of
caste in the little town. I should much prefer something on the principle of the Public Library in Chicago or any other large city, and above all an institution similar to the Peter Cooper Institute of
New York, where everything is plain but neat and
clean and where everything is offered free, in the
way of library, instruction, lectures, art school and
scientific classes.

I believe such a building as this would accomplish
great good, and I believe in connection with an institution of this character there ought to be a room
where men may congregate and chat with each other,

and where, for the benefit of young men, there should be games such as checkers, chess, etc. Many a young man here would be saved from the influence of the Kensington saloons. Pullman is a prohibition town, and this is a commendable feature, but lying on the outskirts of the town, within a few moments' walk of the Arcade, are to be found thirty or thirty-five saloons.

Before we leave the Arcade we might call on Col. Doty, whose office is on the second story. Col. Duane Doty is the editor of the *Pullman Journal*, and the historian and statistician of the Pullman Company. He has a profound admiration for the system upon which the town, is based. He brings to bear his time and talents in the dissemination of literature complimentary to the Pullman Company; all friends visiting the town, sent by Mr. Pullman, are taken on their tour of inspection by Mr. Doty. Charming as a conversationalist and better acquainted with all the details of the business than any other man in the community, he invariably sends the visitor away with most delightful impressions of the town. "A town," in a word, "from which all that is ugly, discordant and demoralizing is eliminated, and which was built as a solution of the industrial problem based upon the idea of mutual recognition." Passing out of the Arcade building, we move east, along "Arcade Row," composed of a block of very pretty nine room cottages, at the extreme east end of which is the home of Mayor Hopkins. On our right is a beau-

tiful little park, tastefully decorated with flowers and
shrubbery; in the center of which is the band stand,
where the Pullman band on summer evenings dis-
courses sweet music, while in the distance can be
seen the Florence Hotel, where, we are told by the
Evening Post, "The aristocracy of Pullman hold forth."
Standing on the corner of Arcade Row, looking east,
is the "Green Stone Church," so named on account
of the color of the stone out of which the structure is
built.   As a piece of ecclesiastical architecture it is
perfection from the outside, but for practical
church purposes it is useless, being composed of one
large room, the auditorium, and three small rooms
at the rear. It has no separate Sunday School room,
parlors, class room or any of the modern conveniences
now found in churches.   A little story is told in regard
to this church which is interesting. In the early history of the town the church stood idle because of the
enormous rent. The Methodists, under the pastorate
of F. W. Warne, now in India, waited on Mr. Pullman with the Rev. Dr. Luke Hitchcock and Bishop
X. Ninde, to rent the church.   Their object was to
get the church at a less rental than was asked at that
time, which was $300.00 a month.   After presenting
all their arguments, Mr. Pullman absolutely refused,
and furthermore said that "when that church was built
it was not intended so much for the moral and spir-
itual welfare of the people as it was for the completion of the artistic effect of the scene." When Mr. Pull-

man built the church, it was his idea that there should
be one church in the town and that all should worship there, but that was impossible. The Roman Cath-
olics received the right by a lease of ninety-nine years
to build a church across the tracks on a large open
prairie, the property of the Pullman Company. The
Swedish Lutherans were permitted to do the same.
The Green Stone Church was finally rented to the
Presbyterians for $100.00 per month; water, steam,
and gas extra. Next to the church and a part of
it is a handsome parsonage, but no minister has
ever been able to live in it, on account of the
high rent of $65 per month. They have had a varied
experience and are now without a settled pastor.
It was in this church that the Rev. Doctor Oggel,
then supplying the church, delivered a sermon eulogis-
tic of Mr. Pullman's great service to his age, his
country, and his town, from the text: "Thou
hast made him a little lower than the angels,
and hast crowned him with glory and honor;" concluding with a quotation from a St. Louis paper,
that Mr. Pullman is worthy of the nomination to the
Presidency of the United States. Dr. Oggel delivered his last sermon on the Sunday after the strike,
in which he declared to the men that "a half
loaf was better than no loaf," and that in his judgment
they were receiving "two-thirds of a loaf."

The M. E. church worships in a large room in
what is known as the Casino building. It is com-

fortable, seated with 326 opera chairs. In the rear are two small rooms, one of which is used for the pastor's study. For these accommodations we pay the Company $300 in rent, $60 in steam, and gas sufficient to bring the amount up to $480.00; to this janitor's services may be added, making the yearly expenditures over $500. The churches could not afford to pay these enormous rents if the people of Pullman were not generous in their support of them.

Leaving the Green Stone Church, going eastward, we come to the Market Hall, a building set apart for such stores as general merchandise. All the stores in the town are rented by individuals who are supposed to be independent of the Company. You are not compelled to purchase at these stores.

As we pass through the Market Hall we go toward Fulton Street. The streets are named after the great inventors, Fulton, Stephenson, Watt, Morse, and Pullman. On Fulton Street are the great tenement blocks, lettered from A to J, three stories, where from 300 to 500 persons live under one roof. These blocks are divided into tenements of two rooms, three rooms and four rooms apiece. These tenements are mostly occupied by foreigners. They are comparatively clean, having air and light; but abundance of water they have not, there being but one faucet for each group of five families, and in some cases the water is in the same apartment devoted to the closets.   There are no yards except a great barren space in common.

Away toward the south of town is the eyesore of the place, known as the brick yards, four rows of little wooden shanties. They are sixteen by twenty feet, ceiling seven feet, a sitting room and two bedrooms, and a kitchen in a lean-to. These cabins could be built easily for $100.00 apiece, and they rent for $8.00 per month or $96.00 a year. The average population of Pullman is about 12,000. It has reached as high as 14,000. The shops are in the center of the town, a large part of the resident portion extending north of the shops. At this end of town are the Rolling Mills, Freight Shops and the Foundry. The whole impression of the town, outside of the central part, is that it is crowded and unwholesome. The houses are all built in solid brick rows. The monotony and regularity of the buildings give one the impression that he is living in soldiers' barracks. There is no such thing as a home in the American sense of the word; owing to the high rents hundreds of families having two or three room apartments, keep boarders and roomers, striving in this way to add to the earnings of the head of the family, to make both ends meet.

During the past winter it took the earnings of both host and boarder to pay the rent and keep above the plain of destitution. In no community in the world, probably, is there such a small proportion of families which really live in family privacy. In the north end of town there are rows of houses where there is no front door for the family living upstairs. They are required to pass through the alley into the yard, up a back stair to reach their homes. In some parts of the town there are houses where, if you desire to reach the family living upstairs, you are compelled, night or day, to pass through the apartments of the family on the lower floor. This destroys the sanctity of the home and is not conducive to the morality of the town. Indeed, as I know to be a fact, the morals of Pullman are not up to the standard that they might be.

An unpleasant feature of the town is that you are made to feel at every turn the presence of the corporation. As Peter Quinon, of the Pittsburg Times, well says: "The corporation is everything and everywhere. The corporation trims your lawn and attends to your trees; the corporation sweeps your street, and sends a man around to pick up every cigar stump, every bit of paper, every straw or leaf; the corporation puts two barrels in your back yard, one for ashes and one for refuse of the kitchen; the corporation has the ashes and refuse hauled away; the corporation provides you new barrels when the others are worn out; the corporation does practically everything but sweep your room and make your bed, and the corporation expects you to enjoy it and hold your tongue." This is a corporation made and a corporation governed town, and is utterly un-American in its tendencies.

The great trouble with this whole Pullman system is that it is not what it pretends to be. No one can but admire many of the beautiful features of this town. To the casual visitor it is a veritable paradise—to the passing student of the industrial problem, it has a fascinating appearance; but like the play, there is a good deal of tinsel and show about it. It is a sort of hollow mockery, sham, an institution girdled with red tape, and as a solution of the labor problem a very unsatisfactory one. The great trouble with the town, viewed from the standpoint of an industrial experiment, is that while it possesses some excellent features, still its deficiencies overbalance all its beauties. It belongs to the map of Europe. It is a civilized relic of European serfdom. We all enjoy living here because there is an equality of interest, and we have a common enemy, the Company, but our daily prayer is, "Lord, keep us from dying here." An eminent writer in Harper's Monthly, in 1884, on "Pullman," declared that at that time, ten years ago, its great faults were: "Bad administration in respect to the employment, retention and promotion of employees. Change is constant in men and officers, and each new superior appears to have his own friends, whom he appoints to desirable positions. Favoritism and nepotism exist; natural dissatisfaction, a powerful prevalence of petty jeal-

ousies, discouragements of superior excellence, fre-
quent change of residents, and an all-pervading feeling of insecurity." The writer further declares that
it is not an American idea. It is a species of benevolent feudalism, and as to its morals, the writer says:
"The prevailing tendency at that day was, 'The desire to beat the company.'"

It seems to me that the town has not changed.
What a commentary on the present state of affairs!
To-day we behold the lamentable and logical out-
come of the whole system. If this town was established with the hope of bettering the relations of Capital and Labor, then I believe it has partially failed
in its mission, and will never succeed until some of
its conditions are changed.

CHAPTER III.

Suffer a word regarding Mr. Pullman himself. I would like to pay my respects to him. I have nothing to say of him that savors of fulsome eulogy or nauseating praise. When I consider him as a man, and hold him up to the youth of our land as an example, I find many things worthy of consideration. All honor to Mr. Pullman for the magnificent business sagacity in the development of the Pullman palace car idea. Few men are capable of bringing to a successful issue such marvelous results. It is no small thing for one man to be able to create a vast productive industry, which is one of the century's civilizing strides, and which, from a small beginning, has reached a market value of $50,000,000. It takes brain to do that sort of thing, and Mr. Pullman as a financier is one of the brainiest men of his day.

In this age of rapidly increasing fortunes, when men become rich in a day by speculation, weaving a fabric of success upon the ruin of others, I am willing to accord honor to a man who has become rich as the result of the establishment of a great manufacturing industry. As a man of industry, possessed of a

27

great idea and tenacioulsy clinging to that idea until he has wrought it out to completion, rising as a poor boy in an obscure village, to a great position as a business man, possessed no doubt with a desire to better his fellow-man, retaining a personal character which, we have every reason to believe, is honest and pure, he is an example in these things that we can hold up before the youth of our land, and bid them imitate.

But when Mr. Pullman, as a public man, stands before the world and demands of us that we regard him as a benefactor to his race, as a true philanthropist, as one who respects his fellow-men, who regards his employees with the love of a father for his children, and would have us associate him with such men as George Peabody, Peter Cooper and George W. Childs, I confess as a clergyman, delivering this message under the shadow of these deserted shops, I fail utterly to see the point. The facts are not in harmony with the requirements demanded.

No man craves Mr. Pullman's position before the American people to-day. He stands in an unenviable light before the world, an example to others of his kind to beware lest they make the same sad mistake. The very qualities that made him successful in life, have, untempered with nobler elements, placed him in his present predicament before the American public. Determination and resolution have turned into arrogance and obstinacy. The same disposition that has kept him aloof in all these months and years of the past from the active life of his town and estranged him from the heart of his employees, is indicated in the cold and arrogant language of his ultimatum when appealed to by President and Mayor and public in general—"Nothing to arbitrate." What a golden opportunity this gentleman has had in the past years of his life to immortalize himself in the hearts of his countrymen, to work out some problem in the solution of the industrial question, to advance the true interest of his city and his country, and yet how utterly has he failed!

As all the facts come to light, it is plain that Mr. Pullman could have prevented the great strike, with its attendant consequences, without sacrificing either his dignity or his money. Appealed to by the city, state, and federal government, while thousands of dollars' worth of property was being destroyed, and the trade of half the country was paralyzed, human lives were being sacrificed, and bloody riot hung like a pall over the city and country, nevertheless this gentleman, having fled from the scene of action, in his secure and comfortable retreat by the seashore, absolutely refused to make even a formal concession.

The odium of his position will never leave Mr. Pullman. So utterly wrong was his attitude that it is no wonder that he has reaped the censure and universal condemnation of the press and public opinion of the country. He can never recover from the

moral effects of his untenable and unpatriotic action.
That the reader may thoroughly understand this
matter I quote from the New York World of July
14th, 1894:

"On Monday a committee of Mr. Pullman's working
men, accompanied by members of the city council,
and with the approval of Mayor Hopkins, waited
upon his representative and offered to submit the
question of whether or not there was anything to arbitrate to a committee composed of two members
chosen by himself (Mr. Pullman), two selected by the
circuit judges of Cook County, and one to be chosen
by these four. Laboring men were to have no representative on the committee, yet they pledged themselves to abide by its decision. This offer, which was
practically a surrender by the men, was perempto-
rily rejected by Mr. Pullman's telegraphic order on
the ground that 'he will not permit outsiders to run
his business.'

"Alderman McGillen's criticism upon this arrogant
and unpatriotic attitude is perfectly sound. He re-
minds Mr. Pullman that the Company and other corporations of the land are quasi-public corporations
which have enjoyed public benefits from the community. He points out that the principal asset of
the Pullman Company is its list of patents, and that
that asset has been conferred by the nation. He
argues logically that a corporation enjoying millions
as the fruit of such public benefit owes something to
the public, especially where the preservation of peace
is involved."

As the champion of labor, standing in direct contrast to Mr. Pullman, is Mr. Eugene V. Debs, President of the American Railway Union. Mr. Debs is
an American of French parentage, thirty-nine years

of age, born in Terre Haute, Indiana.   He is a man
of great executive ability and a wonderful organizer.
He possesses a rare gift of oratory, good voice and
presence, magnetic and earnest.   Educated in the
public schools of Terre Haute, he has ever retained
his love of study and is a great reader.   When sixteen years old, he began life as a painter in the Van-
dalia Railroad shops.   Later he was fireman upon
the same road.   Entering public life, he was elected
to the office of city clerk of Terre Haute, and later
served two terms as member of the state legislature.
For fourteen consecutive years he filled the office of
grand secretary and treasurer of the Brotherhood of
Locomotive Firemen. Always an earnest advocate
of a federation of railway men, he conceived the idea
of the American Railway Union, which came into
existence in this city, June 20th, 1893. I have heard
Mr. Debs speak several times, have conversed with
him, watched him preside over the deliberations of
the late convention of the A. R. U.   I believe he is
thoroughly sincere in the cause he advocates, a born
leader, deliberate and self-possessed, somewhat of an
enthusiast, a man of more than ordinary ability.
I make no apology for his attitude in the matter of
the "boycott,"except that he was forced by the logic of
his position into his fight with the Railroad Managers.
Mr. Debs needs no word from me. He is fully capable of taking care of himself.   Mistaken he may have
been as to his methods, but sincere he is as to the

cause of labor. Mr. Pullman was obstinate, Mr. Debs determined. I know that Debs has always counseled moderation, and positively demanded of his followers to commit no violence. Had all the strikers been of like mind, and had the mob elements, the rabble, and cheap foreign labor imported to this country by such gentlemen as the Railroad Managers, not taken advantage of the situation to commit violence, the condition of things would have been different. Until the American people will recognize the true merits of the laboring man's position and demands, until corporations shall cease to be tyrannical and millionaires arrogant, until there shall be more of the love of God and love for fellow-man in the hearts of rich and poor alike, then, and not till then, will society be rid of such men as Pullman and the mission of such as Mr. Debs will cease.

After the smoke of battle shall have rolled away, and the public mind regains its equanimity, I believe the calm verdict of the American people concerning this man will be very different from that engendered by a rabid and capitalistic press.

CHAPTER IV.

HISTORY OF THE STRIKE.

Let us review briefly the history of the strike.
From August, 1892, to August, 1893, was a season
of unwonted prosperity and activity in the Pullman
shops. It is safe to say that four hundred new Pullman cars were added to the service. During the
winter of 1893 the magnificent train of Pullman cars
exhibited at the World's Fair was built. Work was
abundant, wages fair, and the force of employees in
creased to between five and six thousand. Then came
the reaction and depression of trade. The force was
gradually reduced until late in the summer not over
900 men were employed. About November of 1893,
Mr. Pullman began to secure contracts for new work,
and the cars which had been out on the road in the
World's Fair traffic were rapidly brought into the
shops for repairs. The force was enlarged until, during the winter, from three to four thousand employees
were on the pay roll. Then commenced the cutting
of wages, and consequent abuse on the part of the
local administration complained of so bitterly by the
men. Mutterings of dissatisfaction, discontent and
continual resentings of petty abuses were heard on all

sides during the long and bitter winter. "There will be trouble in the spring," was an expression which I heard on all sides. Destitution prevailed to a great extent. Want and suffering was no uncommon picture. As a pastor I came in contact directly with much suffering. Repeated cutting of the wages with no corresponding reduction of rent exasperated the employees. I was aware that the men were being organized into local unions. Hearing of the success of the American Railway Union, and casting about for some one to champion their cause, these unions appealed to Messrs. Debs and Howard of the American Railway Union.

Meetings were held at Kensington. Messrs. Debs and Howard repeatedly counseled the men not to strike, but to wait until the American Railway Union had acquired strength, and agreed in due season to assist the men in their effort to obtain redress from their wrongs. At this juncture a committee waited on Manager Middleton. Meeting with no favorable response, they appointed a committee and waited on Vice-President Wickes at the city offices. Mr. Wickes received the committee very kindly, listened to their grievances and promised that Mr. Pullman would give them a final answer the following week. On the day appointed, the committee again appeared at the city office, where Mr. Pullman delivered to them his first statement, with which the public is familiar. In that statement he refused to accede to the demand of the

employees for a restoration of the scale of wages for
1893, on the ground that he had taken contracts for
new work at a loss. As proof thereof he agreed to
permit an inspection of his books. He stated further
that he could not reduce the rents of his houses. He
agreed that none of the committee waiting on him
should be discharged, and also stated that their grievances should be investigated So far, so good. But
the employees were disappointed and chagrined. I
well remember that we who were residents of the
town, not in the employ of the company, and anxious
to see the threatened strike averted, breathed easier
that night, but still were apprehensive. Anxiously
we awaited the morrow. What caused the disap-
pointment and chagrin of the employees? It was
this. Mr. Pullman had given out that he had taken
contracts for new work at a loss, because out of love
for his employees he desired to keep the shops open.
Unfortunately the men had never seen any evidences
of paternal love on the part of Mr Pullman in his
previous dealings with them, and they could not dis-
abuse their minds of the thought that perhaps he was
keeping the shops open, and taking work at a loss in
order to get his returns in rent. Also they felt that
his refusal to reduce their rents was unjust. They
were suspicious and in no condition to be trifled
with. I am sure Mr. Pullman had no idea of the true
state of affairs and did not fully realize how unjustly
his employees had been dealt with, and the magni-

tude of the petty annoyances to which they had been subjected.

On the morrow, three men who were members of the committee were "laid off." While it was no uncommon thing in the shops for men to be "laid off," still it had come to be looked upon as amounting in many cases to a virtual discharge.

Cases have been cited to me of employees, who, having incurred the displeasure of those in authority, were "laid off," and returning again and again for work found that they were really discharged. What made the matter worse in this case was that the men laid off discovered that it was the direct action of the acting superintendent's retaliations upon them for complaints uttered by them against him the day previous at the city meeting. The discharge of these men was resented by the whole committee as a violation of Mr. Pullman's agreement with them.

Furthermore, the grievances were investigated during the day, but were investigated on an *ex parte* basis. The committee of investigation was composed, among others, of Vice-President Wickes, General Manager Brown, Manager Middleton, Chief Accountant Wilde, Mr. Campbell of the Repair department and Mr. Runnells, leading counsel for the company. No one appeared as a committee of defense for the men, to see that their side was duly represented. The grievances were made light of and treated as trivial and inconsequential. Three men stated to me personally that as they each came out of the Manager's office they respectively felt, to use their own language, like a "set of fools."

In this condition of things, the employees met that night (Thursday) in a secret all-night session composed of about forty-six men representing the different local unions. They voted unanimously, in view of the unsatisfactory treatment they had received at the hands of the Company, to strike the following Saturday. It seems that in their midst was a spy; their deliberations and decision reached the ears of the company early Friday morning. They went to work at 7 A. M. Abut 9 A. M., intelligence was conveyed to the leaders that their action was known to the company and that the company had decided to lock up the shops at the noon hour. It is claimed by the men (whether true or not I do not know) that a telegram from the city to lock up, was intercepted by an operator in sympathy with the employees and thus the word was given to them. Rather than have a "lock-out" the men passed the word from one to another to "walk out," which they did orderly and deliberately. About six hundred remained until the noon hour, a few returned until the evening, when notices were posted on the shop gates to the effect that the shops would be closed indefinitely and the works closed down. Thus began the great Pullman strike.

CHAPTER V.

CHARACTER AND INCIDENTS OF THE STRIKE.

From the 11th of May, 1894, until the present writing (July 23rd, 1894) the Pullman strike has been a remarkable exhibition of orderliness and correct deportment. It has been a "model strike" so far as Pullman is concerned. Up to the evening of July 5th, in the seventh week of the strike, not the slightest unusual infringement of law had taken place. The universal comment was complimentary to the decorum of the strikers. For seven weeks the town was quieter than at any other time in its history, less drinking, less roystering, less noise, not even an occasional fisticuffs encounter to enliven the monotony of events. Even the patrol forgot to tear madly through our streets as of old.

No wonder, for the strike leaders gave out repeatedly at their nightly meetings that order would be positively enforced, and warning was given to keep clear of the saloons in Kensington and Roseland. So determined were the men that the property of the Company should not be molested that they offered to place a cordon of men around the shops to protect them. On the evening of the 5th of July, when the

"Boycott" of the American Railway Union against the Pullman cars was at its height, the Illinois Central railway having decided to run the mail train known as the "Diamond Special," some difficulty occurred at the Kensington depot, which resulted in the stopping of the train. Later in the evening (about midnight) a mob of hoodlums and fellows of the "baser sort" arriving from South Chicago, set fire to a number of Illinois Central freight cars about a mile north of Pullman. The next morning a mob of the same character gathered at Kensington, marched past Pullman on the railroad track and overturned box cars. A United States deputy by the name of Stark fired wildly into the crowd. William Anslyn, an innocent spectator about 250 feet from the scene, was shot. Falling upon his face, he endeavored to rise, when Stark, according to the deposition of eye witnesses, advanced and deliberately fired a shot into the back of the prostrate man. Two days thereafter Anslyn died, as the result of the brutal deed. The deputy is still at large.

Infuriated by this deed, the mob endeavored to lay hands on the deputy marshal, but he was saved by the interposition of the police. Great excitement prevailed. Threatenings of every description filled the air; rumors of various kinds floated all day through the town. In the afternoon more cars near Burnside were set on fire. In the evening the militia arrived in Pullman and have remained to date. The presence of the militia was salutary at the time, but their long continued presence and the martial law to which the town has been subjected, I believe, has had a demoralizing effect upon the community. With all due respect to the noble boys in blue, I yet believe that order could have been sustained by the local authorities, and the moral conservatism of the best elements among the strikers and citizens.

An interesting feature of the strike has been the regular daily public meeting. For the first two weeks these public gatherings were held afternoon and evening. The afternoon meetings were dispensed with, the meetings confined to the evening. The proprietors of the Turner Hall, capable of accommodating an audience of 800 to 1,000 persons, generously donated the use of the room free of charge. As the weather became warmer the meetings were held in the open air, on an adjoining lot, a rude platform having been improvised out of some old dry goods boxes. Here, night after night, immense audiences have gathered to listen to addresses from speakers good, bad and indifferent. It was an open platform, free for all, and many splendid addresses have been delivered to the assembled strikers. All classes of speakers were allowed to address the multitude, among them several clergymen. The chairman, Mr. Heathcote, endeavored as far as possible to curb the utterances of those who became too radical in their fiery denunciation of the wrongs perpetrated upon the laborer by grinding corporations and monopolistic combinations of wealth.

Early in the strike, the conduct of affairs was vested in a committee known as the Central Strike Committee, composed of members of each of the local unions. Mr Heathcote is the chairman of the committee, Mr. R. W. Brown Vice-President, and Mr. John Berry, Secretary. As chairman of this committee and as the representative spokesman of the strikers, it is no more than fair to bespeak the highest praise for Mr. Heathcote, for the calm and care ful manner in which he has performed the onerous duties of his office. He and his assqciates have all earned the good will of the general public of this and the surrounding community, in endeavoring to preserve order and decorum in the ranks of their followers.

By far the most important feature of the strike has been that of the Relief Committee, organized immediately after the strike commenced. It has been in active service ever since, and is the center of attraction to the vast army of strikers and their families. Of this committee Mr. Frank Pollans is the obliging and effective chairman;Mr.J.J.Maguire the thoroughly competent assistant; Miss May Woods has proved herself to be an untiring and accomplished secretary, and Mr. David V. Gladman, the trusted and efficient treasurer. Associated with these friends has been a well equipped and devoted corps of workers of every description, whose energies have been taxed to their utmost to meet the demands of their hungry and necessitous fellows.

When the committee was organized, a call was sent forth for food and money. The firm of Secord and Hopkins of Kensington, of which Mayor Hopkins is a partner, was the first to respond with the magnificent gift of 25,000 pounds of flour, 25,000 pounds of meat, and the use for the benefit of the strikers of a room above their store free of rent for the committee on care of the sick so long as the strike lasted. At the same time a committee of ladies interested in the cause of labor, led on by Mrs. Fanny Clarke Kavanagh and Mrs. Dr. Charles D. Bradley of Chicago, opened a store donated by the proprietors of the Chicago Daily News, as the city headquarters for the Pullman Strikers' Relief Fund.

From that day to this, from Chicago and all the country, have come daily contributions of relief in cash and provisions. The response of the public to this fund has been remarkable, and has indicated the widespread practical sympathy aroused through the country on behalf of the suffering employees. Among the cash contributions will be found amounts from twenty-five cents to a thousand dollars Among the larger cash contributions may be noted: Typographical Union No 16, $1,000; the A. A. of I. & S. Workers, Lakeside Lodge No. 9, $686; Painters and Decorators Union No. 147, $500; Carpenters'

Union No. 23, $100; Carpenter's Union No. 1, $100;
Thirty-fourth Ward Republican Club, $101; the people
of Hammond, Indiana, $500; Carpenters' Union of
Englewood, $100; United Turner Societies of Pull-
man, Kensington, and Roseland, $400; Western
Avenue Sewer Men, $77.50; Chicago Ticket Brokers'
Association, $78; Chicago Typographical Union,
$200; Grand Crossing Police, $46; Hyde Park Water
Department, $29; Wood's Circus, $30; Picnic at
Gardener's Park, $15.38; Milk Dealer's Union, $85;
Hyde Park Liquor Dealers, $25; Fourteenth Pre-
cinct Police Station, $43; Spiegel's Home Furnish-
ing Company, $20; "The Leader," Chicago, $100;
"The Hub," Chicago, $200. The most princely gift
among the down-town establishments was that of
Siegel, Cooper & Co., who gave 200 barrels of flour.
Brewers and Maltsters' Union No. 18, $50; Swedish
Concert, $50; Local Union 553, Fernwood, $78.25;
Chicago Fire Department, $909.75; German Sing-
ing Society, $140; cheque from Anaconda, Mont.,
$250.

The donations of provisions have been legion;
everything imaginable, from a bottle of ink to a car
load of flour. No delicacies or luxuries, but the sub-
stantials of life were given in abundance. Among
the articles donated may be mentioned innumerable
sacks of flour, hams, potatoes, coffee, peas, soap,
milk, meat, one caddy of chewing tobacco and seven
pounds of smoking tobacco to solace the minds of

anxious strikers. From two firms came boxes of shirts, and one Oppenheimer, realizing that strikers must not go hatless, donated a box of hats.

To these gifts of cash and provisions must be added the care of the sick. Three hundred dollars has already been spent for the care of the sick. In case of death the burial expenses are paid if necessary. Certain physicians of Pullman and surrounding towns have kindly given their services free of charge, and most of the druggists have given donations of medicine. To summarize, the total amount of money (not including provisious) given to the Relief Fund up to July 21st, 1894, was $15,-000.00, the total expenses to same date, $14,000.00, leaving a balance in the treasury of $1,000,00. Besides this, Mr. S. Keliher, Secretary of the A. R. U., has another $1,000 subject to the order of the local Central Committee. In the distribution of provisions, the greatest care has been taken to see that justice is equally dispensed to all. At this writing, 2,700 families are being provided for, counting six to a family.

Some minor features of the strike may be noted. It has naturally caused endless discussions pro and con among the residents of the "model town." Class distinctions have always been a marked feature of the little community, and the influence of the strike has only served to intensify these distinctions. Outside of the great mass of the employees and their families there is a little coterie of individuals termed

in a late edition of the Chicago Evening Post, the
aristocratic element of the town, whose headquarters
may be called the beautiful little hostelry known as
the Florence Hotel. Here the officials and the elite
of the community assemble and discuss the situation.
Soon after the white ribbons were donned by the
striking employees and their sympathizers as sug-
gested by Mr. Debs, those who were opposed to the
strike wore a miniature American flag. Does this
mean that they who wore the flag indicate thereby
that the striking employees are un-American endorsers
of lawlessness and anarchy? Does it mean that the
Pullman strikers are treasonable in their attitude of
a quiet and determined demand for justice and a fair
wage? Let it be remembered that no corresponding town of its size in the country can boast of more
well organized, active, patriotic societies than the
town of Pullman,—the G. A. R., the P. O. S. of
A., the P. O. D. of A., the Sons of Veterans, etc.
There is as much if not more patriotic fervor for the
old flag and American institutions to the square inch
in Pullman than in any other town in the country.
And who is it that compose these organizations? It
is these very men and their wives and daughters who
are known as the Pullman strikers. As for me, I would
rather wear the white ribbon with the American flag
over it—American labor protected by the stars and
stripes in its demand for justice from the inhumanity
of grasping corporations. My friend Rev. F. Atch-

ison, pastor of the Hyde Park M. E. Church of Chicago, spoke truly at a late mass meeting when he said, referring to this subject, "The American flag ought to be the best guaranty that an honest day's work should receive an honest day's pay. If any one class more than another was entitled to wear and carry the American flag, it was the workingman. The men who had borne the flag to victory in the late war were American workingmen. They won freedom for all." The speaker said that if ever he went on a strike he would wear both the white ribbon and the American flag. At Pullman he had seen the white ribbon and the G. A. R. button on the same breast, and both emblems were in good company. These are true words, and it may be well to add that there are thirty-seven old soldiers among the Pullman strikers who wear the Grand Army button.

CHAPTER VI.

So peculiar are the relations of the Pullman Company to the town of Pullman and its employees that it is not an easy task to one unfamiliar with the situation to point out the sophistries and misleading points in Mr. Pullman's statements to the public. A Chicago man, who is a well known writer for the press, remarked to me after carefully looking over the ground, that it would be a very easy matter to write up a strong argument in favor of the Pullman Company; and on the other hand, an easy matter to make out a strong case in favor of the employees. But to give a fair and impartial statement, showing wherein the Company had dealt wrongly with its employees, required a thorough knowledge of the situation.

This is true. There are three statements before the public from the Pullman Company's standpoint. The first was given on May 9th by Mr. Pullman to his employees, in answer to their committee, who waited on him two days before the strike.

The second was given to the public on June 12th by the Company, just previous to the putting into

47

effect of the boycott on the Pullman cars by the American Railway Union, and the third statement was given on July 13th by Mr. Pullman himself under date of New York, in defense of his attitude in refusing to arbitrate. These statements are all so plausible upon their face that I am not at all surprised that so many have been inclined to criticise the action of the employees and endorse the apparently magnanimous position of the Company.

Furthermore, the attitude of the Chicago press has been such as to completely bewilder the thoughtful and intelligent citizen who desires to know the truth, and to poison the minds of that element in our midst whose sympathies naturally gravitate to the side of wealth.

I presume that if I had lived in Chicago instead of Pullman, and knew nothing about the Pullman strike except what I read in three of the leading Chicago newspapers, I would have raised my hand in holy horror against these wicked Pullman strikers and all belonging to their side, and would have sustained Mr. Pullman and his company.

But living as I do in Pullman, having studied the situation carefully for two years, and being absolutely independent of the company and employees, I know enough to enable me to read between the lines of these beautiful Pullman statements and note the fallacies of their position.

I hold Mr. Pullman responsible for the whole situation by virtue of his presidency of the company, and the marvelous influence he exercises over the whole Pullman system. He is the King, and he demands to the full measure of his capacity all that belongs to the insignia of royalty. It is about as difficult for an ordinary man, one of his employees, to see Mr. Pullman as for a subject of Russia to see the Czar. Every official of his company is absolutely subject to his authority. He expects it. He will have it. I have been surprised to hear those who have sat in his presence describe the lordly manner in which he treats even those who are nearest to the throne. Sometimes he meets with gentlemen among his officials who object to this subserviency. Instances have been related to me of gentlemen who have rebelled against Mr. Pullman's absolutism and resigned rather than endure it. Of course this is Mr. Pullman's right, but it seems to me that imperialism on the part of a gentleman so powerful in influence as Mr. Pullman is unpleasant to say the least, and capable of producing harm whether intentional or not toward those in authority under him. It is unfortunate to work for a corporation realizing that if you once dispute the will of the king, off goes your head. Imperialism on the part of the king, breeds imperialism in the court. Even subordinates become infected with the disease, and great harm is thereby produced among the subjects If the public will reflect upon this they will see how, under a system like that upon which Pullman is founded, great dissatisfaction can easily be produced among the employees. Upon careful examination I find in conversation with the employees that one half the trouble in the shops has been produced by unfair and tyrannical dealing on the part of certain foremen and others in the local administration. Mr. Pullman certainly must be aware of these things, and, if so, why did he not see that they were remedied long ago? If he did not hear of or know these things, then somebody has either willfully misrepresented the true state of affairs to him, or colored the statements to suit themselves. I am in a position to know that information of everything going on in the town of Pullman, social, political, shop talk, town talk of any importance, and so on, is conveyed by letter every week to headquarters from the town proper. I have no objection to that. But still I don't like it. I accept it as a peculiarity of the system upon which the town is established. For instance, during my first year as pastor a certain unfortunate occurrence took place in connection with a gentleman, a member of my church and an employee. Before the week was out, I was roused from my sleep one night by a gentleman in the employ of the Company, who, in the presence of my wife and myself, took a stenographic report of the affair. The gentleman informed me that it was necessary to have a correct report so that he could embody it in his regular weekly letter to the president. That was

an eye-opener to me.   I dislike espionage.   But as
long as it is a part of the system, it's all right, and
I will not complain.   But it produces unpleasant re-
flections.

From this standpoint, I hold Mr. Pullman responsible for the situation.   But while I do so, I am ready
to allow that perhaps he was not cognizant of the
true state of affairs from the reason assigned above.
I do not hesitate, however, to place a large measure
of responsibility upon the general and local management.   The authority vested in officials of such a
large corporation as this, gives opportunity for the
exercise of great power.   When a few officials are
given the right to employ or discharge men, to set
the prices of labor and to decide a thousand questions
concerning the details of a vast business indissolubly
connected with the welfare and financial prospects of
3,000 men, I contend that such officials should be absolutely free from favoritism, tyrannical dealing, or
unfairness.   While I make all allowance for motives
of jealousy and anger, still I submit it to the public
and to the directors and president of the Company,
if it be not reasonable to believe that favoritism, tyranny and unfairness do exist in the local manage-
men, when 2,000 men universally declare such to be
the case.

Let us note some points in Mr. Pullman's statements.   *Point I.*—He says:

"A little more than a year ago the shops at Pullman were in a prosperous condition; work was plenty, wages were high and the condition of the employees was indicated by the fact that the local savings bank had of savings deposits nearly $700,000, of which nearly all was the property of the employees."

"A little more than a year ago" would take us back to June, 1893. According to the Report of the Pullman Loan & Savings Bank for July 25, 1893, as published in the Pullman Journal, the official organ of the Pullman Company, there was in liabilities, the following:

Capital stock paid in.............$	100,000.00
Surplus fund....................	75,000.00
Undivided profits................	27,252.83
Savings deposits subject to notice...	631,354.25
Individual deposits subject to check.	368,365.76
Demand certificates of deposit......	2,538.26
Certified checks.................	40.00
Cashier's checks outstanding.......	2,972.94

Total....................$1,207,524.04

According to the above, there is a slight difference between Mr. Pullman's $700,000 and the bank statement on "Savings deposits." Merely a matter of $68,-645.75. Now the question arises, was the $631,354.25 entirely the amount deposited by the employees, mechanics and laborers? It is a well known fact that some of the officials are depositors in the local bank. The salaries of these gentlemen are large, many of the heads of departments draw good pay, and these naturally deposit in this bank. Furthermore, the local storekeepers are depositors also.

Many storekeepers in Roseland, Kensington and Gano deposit therein, also treasurers of lodges. One gentleman in the employ of the company is said to have $30,000.00 deposited. I am acquainted with one employee, who informed me that he sold his farm in an adjacent state before coming here, and deposited $3,000.00 therein. If all or any of this was counted as the savings of employees, then it would be comparatively easy to make such a glowing statement. While I presume that part of the above enumerated items were credited as "individual deposits subject to check," still I hold that some of them were credited to "savings" deposits. And further, there are many working people not employed by the Pullman Company who place "savings deposits" in the Pullman Bank because of its reliability.

If, for illustration, I deposit $10.00 to-day on my own account as savings, and to-morrow deposit $200.00 on my own account, money entrusted to me by my church to meet future expenses, it would not be fair to reckon my account as "savings deposits" of the employees, and base a statement thereon for the general public. As a matter of information, and an interesting fact connected with the subject under discussion, I am informed by a gentleman well qualified to speak, that among the employees, the class who save the most money out of their wages are the common laborers. The foreign element in our midst are far more saving than our native Amer-

ican mechanics.   They live, many of them, as an
American mechanic would not wish to live, and con-
sequently save more money out of their scant earnings
than our mechanics.

Again, if $700,000 indicated the amount actually
belonging to the employees in 1893, then how is it
that they were in arrears, as the Company elsewhere
affirm, $70,000 on rent at the time of the strike, May
1894?   If the employees were worth $700,000 in
August 1893, and in May 1894 had not only drawn it
all out of the bank, but were $70,000 in arrears on
rent besides, it certainly proves that their wages were
so small that they were gradually moving toward the
"starvation wage" point, as affirmed so often by the
employees. I make no pretenses as a financier, but
I know right from wrong.   This statement, thought-
fully pondered by the public, from my point of view
looks serious, when we remember the vast wealth of
this company, the great surplus at its command (for
one year only, 1892, $3,250,389.07), its two per cent
quarterly dividend ($600,000) over and above all ex-
penses, and then think of its cruel cutting of the
wages of its employees.

A visitor came to this town last summer, made his
home at the luxurious Florence Hotel, and forthwith
sat down and wrote a little pamphlet entitled, "The
Story of Pullman," in which, after eulogizing it as a
"town that is bordered with bright beds of flowers
and green velvety stretches of lawn, shaded with

trees, and dotted with parks and pretty water vistas,
and glimpses here and there of artistic sweeps of landscape gardening; a town, in a word, where all that
is ugly and discordant and demoralizing is eliminated,
and all that inspires to self-respect is generously provided," he closes his book stating that the town of
Pullman "has illustrated the helpful combination of
Capital and Labor without strife or stultification,
upon the lines of mutual recognition." This book is
endorsed by the company and is handed to every
visitor to Pullman who desires a copy. Now if, the
times are so depressing as to compel the employees
who have been long faithful to the company to eat
up their little savings, why, if this company believes
in "mutual recognition," do they not themselves bear
a little of this burden of "depressing times?" Why
does not Mr. Pullman stand before his board of directors, who represent the 3,246 stockholders of the
Pullman Company, of which, 1,800 control the funds
of educational and charitable institutions, and of
which 1,494 are women, among them, as we are told,
Her Majesty, Queen Victoria, and demand of them
upon the basis of morality and right that instead of
declaring a quarterly dividend of 2 per cent in
these terribly depressed times, they declare a dividend of one and one-half per cent, and place the
$114,000, representing the other one-half per cent, to
the credit of the pay roll?

This may not be "business," but it would be "mu-

tual recognition." While the Pullman Company claims
on the one hand that its whole system is purely financial, with not one ounce of real philanthropic blood
flowing through its veins (which is certainly true of
its non-arbitrating President), still it has caused thousands of dollars' worth of complimentary literature to
be scattered abroad for these many years, throughout
the country, like the above pamphlet, giving a quasi-
endorsement to the alleged fact that the town is established as a solution of the industrial problem upon
the basis of "mutual recognition." In support of
my position on this matter, I quote entire an edito-
rial taken from the columns of the *Daily Republican*,
of Springfield, Mass., under date of Wednesday, July
11. It hits the nail on the head. It is gratifying to
learn that my position is not altogether Utopian, and
is supported by one of the most reliable journals of
the country:

PULLMAN PROFITS AND WAGES.

"After the smoke of the present battle has cleared
away, the merits of the original controversy between
Mr. Pullman and his employees will remain as a subject of some public inquiry and discussion. Closely
bearing on this point is the financial condition of the
Pullman Company. Its operations for the last two
full fiscal years, ending July 31, resulted as follows:—

	1892.	1893.
Earnings,	$8,061,081	$9,200,685
Royalties, profits, etc.,	1,941,275	2,189,211
Total revenue,	$10,002,356	$11,389,896
Operating expenses,	$3,438,863	$3,825,940
Other expenses,	1,013,104	1,037,508
Dividends on stock,	2,300,000	2,520,000
Surplus,	$3,250,389	$4,006,448

"Thus, after declaring a dividend on the stock of 8 per cent, the company had left a surplus in 1893 large enough to have warranted an extra dividend of over 10 per cent, and in 1892 it could have declared an extra dividend of 8 per cent, above the 8 per cent actually divided. Ever since 1876 this company has paid dividends of from 8 to 9 1-2 per cent, and rare has been the year in which it has not carried a large sum to the surplus account, which in the main has not been invested in the plant of the company, and is presumably available in large part for division among the stockholders—an aggregate sum to date of some $24,000,000, or within $12,000,000 of the entire amount of capital invested from the stock. Mr. Pullman personally is a very wealthy man, said to be worth some $25,000,000.

"This is a very remarkable showing of profits from manufacturing industry. Its parallel for richness is hardly to be found in the country, outside of the sugar trust and one or two other combinations. It cannot be found among the railroads or among any of the ordinary manufacturing or mercantile enterprises. It is the biggest gold mine probably uncovered in the country before the advent of the 'trust' idea.

"When the great strike and riots of 1877 were precipitated by a reduction of 10 per cent in the

wages of the employees of the Baltimore and Ohio
and other roads, Mr. Garrett's company was paying
10 per cent on its stock; and *The Republican* held
at the time that the company should have put at least
a part of the reduction upon capital, reducing the
dividend rate to, say, 9 per cent, after which wages
might be brought into consideration. And at that
time 10 per cent on money was far less above the
general average of rates than it is to-day.

"It may be a question, therefore, for philanthropists
and labor reformers to consider, whether Mr. Pullman, in view of the extraordinary profits he and his
company were accumulating, was or was not morally
bound to share more generously with his men in the
effects of the hard times. He believes in paternalistic
methods, and has put them in operation at his works
to a degree not equaled anywhere else in America.
What could be more in consonance with this policy
than at such a time to dip back into the surplus of
$4,000,000 made in the single previous year and keep
up the wages of employees who are so carefully housed
and otherwise looked after as so many dependents
at Pullman? It may not be true in other cases, but
it is certainly true of such a system of paternalism,
that wage reductions can not be justified in the face
of such profits as the Pullman Company exhibits."

Point 2. Take another item in Mr. Pullman's
statement. He says: "Our pay rolls for that year
(1893) show an average earning of over $600 per an-
num for every person, man, woman or youth, on the
roll."

Following the reasoning adopted above, it might
be asked, Was this estimate based upon the earnings of mechanics and laborers alone? The local

Pullman pay roll is said to include all except the manager and assistant manager. The pay roll includes the large clerical force, heads of departments, all monthly hands, foremen, etc. Then, again, let the general public remember that included in the earnings of these men for 1893 was the immense amount of money earned for *over-time.* The winter of 1893 was one of the busiest in the history of the company. The employees labored day and night. For weeks at a time I did not see the men connected with my church, except on the Sabbath. The employees, of course, were allowed extra pay for the over-time, and this naturally swelled the amount of the pay-roll. This, of course, would make it easy to estimate the above.

Point 3. Mr. Pullman also says in his statement that he took certain contracts for building cars at a loss and that he did so simply to keep his men employed.

There is no doubt and never has been in the minds of his employees that he took certain contracts at a loss. Behind this statement, which has gone forth all over the country, Mr. Pullman has maintained an apparently impregnable position; and the public naturally says: "How can Mr. Pullman pay the wages of 1893, while at the same time he is losing money on certain contracts for building cars?"

But it must be borne in mind that the great bulk of work done in the Pullman shops was the repairing of old cars shipped in from all over the country; cars that had been doing service for the World's Fair traffic. It is safe to say that sixty per cent of the work done in the shops at the time of the strike was repair work, and not new work. The repair work was Mr. Pullman's own work, done by him under contract with the railroad corporations running his cars. When their employees were cut 33 1-3 per cent, in some cases 40 per cent and in others 50 per cent, it was for work done not only on the comparatively small amount of new contracts in the shops, but principally on the repairing of old cars. Furthermore, I understand that a certain amount of this repair work is done at the expense of the railroads running the cars. Of course the company, while it cuts wages, does not repair cars for the roads at a less figure than heretofore on account of "hard times."

Let the public also bear in mind that while the girls employed in the laundry department of the great shops (no small part of the business) were cut in their wages, nevertheless the price of berths on the Pullman Palace cars was not reduced to the general public. If you ate your dinner in a Pullman Palace Car, and wiped your mustache upon a Pullman napkin, laundered by these girls, you did not have to pay less for your dinner as a result of their reduction in wages!

It seems that there is another side of this loss of money on contracts. An interview with one of the brightest men ever in the employ of the Pullman Company, indicates to me that while money has been lost on a few contracts, and wages thereby cut, still thousands of dollars were squandered in the shops last year by mismanagement. For instance, suppose there was a loss per car of a certain amount. It is thought that the system of keeping tally on all lumber used in car construction is faulty. Word comes to change the whole system. That change does not remedy the evil, is, on the contrary, productive of a lot of useless red-tape, and the result is that there is a change that involves a practical loss of $9 to $10 per car. My informant further states that during the winter of 1893, when the shops were running night and day in certain departments, machinery would run for hours without any actual work, merely because of some notion from headquarters. Changes in machinery and constructions of machinery were made, regardless of cost and, in the estimation of my practical informant, unnecessarily. Further, he declares that the engineer's office, departments of estimate and figures on construction of cars, is a useless expense (as it was then run), entailing a drain of $2,000 per month at least on the Company's exchequer. Probably these losses may have had something to do with the reduction of wages. If so, it would have been more just to have laid the responsibility where it belonged and cut gentlemen with high salaries rather than take it out of the "wage-earners."

So peculiar are the methods of the Pullman Company in transacting its business, that the attention of Congress was not long ago called to it by no less a personage than Senator Sherman, of Ohio. To quote the language of a Washington correspondent of the *Inter Ocean*, it seems that the movement was "initiated in the Senate before the strike began, and it had been a subject of serious consideration by Mr. Sherman for many years. He proposes, in short, that the Pullman Company shall be brought within the provisions of the interstate commerce act, and that Congress shall enact a law requiring that corporation to give the public better accommodations at lower rates. He would require the Pullman Company to keep the upper berths up if not sold, and would reduce rates one half. The subject is one as to which there is very likely to be a unanimity of sentiment in Congress. The Pullman Company has so widely advertised its disposition to charge extortionate rates and to refuse to accommodate the public, that if Mr. Sherman shall press his measure, that corporation will find that it will not have a state legislature to deal with."

Senator Sherman said to this correspondent:

"I regard these rates as simply infamous. It is outrageous for us to be compelled to pay such high prices for such poor accommodations as we receive in our trips to and fro about the country. They give you a short, narrow berth, so close and uncomfortable that in many cases one would rather sit up

all night than submit to the inconveniences of the
compartment. If you get a lower berth and no one
has the upper, the porter insists upon putting down
the lid and so increasing your misery rather than
giving you the benefit of the air. I do not know why
this is so, unless it is an effort on the part of the company to make their prestige all the greater and the
more unendurable.

"I regard the Pullman Company and the sugar
trust as the most outrageous monopolies of the day.
They make enormous profits, and give their patrons
little or nothing in return in proportion. It is perfectly clear to me that there is a way to reach the
sleeping-car problem with ease through government
action. States have in many instances adopted reg-
ulations intended to reduce the evil of extortionate
charges on the railroads, but there are few, if any,
railroads that run sleepers through but one state,
and thus these laws are of no avail, tor nc state can
regulate any corporations beyond its own limits.

"The United States can easily control the charges
for sleepers, just as the railway fares have been reg-
ulated by means of the interstate commerce law. I
believe that that act has been amply enforced without
very much trouble, and I can see no reason why a
similar act should not be passed with reference to the
sleeping-car problem. A bill of a dozen lines would
suffice, fixing the rate per mile to be charged by these
companies and providing a penalty for overcharging.
I think the rates should be reduced one-half. The
Pullman Company, for instance, is very rich, made so
by the enormous and disproportionate profits on its
cars. With half that profit the company could make
a great deal of money and give the public better
service.

"Perhaps you do not know, but it is nevertheless
a fact, that the Pullman Company charges each

railroad running its cars a cent a mile for every car, and this goes into the pockets of Pullman in addition to the rates paid by the passenger. For instance, between New York and Chicago the railroad pays about $10 for each sleeper run, and the Pullman Company gets several times that sum in addition from the public. That $10 paid by the railroad is counted into the running expenses of the road, and is eventually paid by the passenger in the fare he gives for his ride. So the traveler pays twice, in reality, for his questionable accommodations on board a sleeper. I feel these heavy rates myself frequently, for when we go out to our home in Ohio we have to pay, for my wife, my daughter and myself, as much for sleeper rates as for the entire railroad fares. The berths are so close and uncomfortable that we have to spread out over a good deal of space in order to avoid being made ill by the journey."

The Senator also referred to the question of tipping as a species of petty extortion. He continued:—

"It is a small matter in the individual case, but it is an extortion to pay the porter for each trip you take. The trouble is that these men are not paid enough by the company. If they were paid adequate salaries the passengers would not be obliged to come forward to help them out. I really think the men need the money in most cases, and I always give, because I do not want to feel or to appear mean about the matter. There is a sort of compulsion about it, though, that is very disagreeable, and it could all be avoided."

Another matter referred to by the Senator is interesting reading:

"There is one matter that should not be overlooked in this consideration. The main patents on these sleepers have expired, and there is no reason why the railroads should not begin now to make and run their own cars. I was acquainted with the original inventor of the sleeping car, who is now dead. He was obliged to sell out to the Pullman Company and they have held the monopoly with great care. The first patents have now, I believe, run out, and although the Pullmans have taken out letters for some improvements, I think it would be perfectly easy for the monopoly to be broken. I think that this abuse can be reached, and I propose to press this matter to some sort of conclusion. It seems to me that the American people have suffered uncomplainingly long enough, especially as there is a remedy at hand."

I may be regarded as presumptuous in quoting as freely from Senator Sherman's interview. The same sentiments have been expressed by the Pullman strikers individually and upon the public platform. But when uttered by a United States Senator they carry with them a weight of influence far beyond that given to them by the poor wage-earner. It is pleasant to have a United States Senator on your side. And, moreover, it is good to quote that powerful journal the *Inter Ocean*, as uttering sentiments in harmony with those entertained by the Pullman strikers. So cruel and fearfully unjust has been the attitude of this newspaper to the labor man and the Pullman employees in particular, during the past nine weeks, that it is like an oasis in the desert to quote it against this grinding and "nothing to arbitrate" corporation.

It seems to me that even if Mr. Pullman did take contracts for new work at a loss, this did not, in view of the foregoing facts, form a valid excuse for the continual cutting of wages. Money was lost, I have no doubt, in prosperous times, not on the net labor and material, but "because afterward a snug sum of 'general expense'—of a fancy plant, salaries of clerks, superintendents, and all attaches of the general office—were thrown into the bill of contract," to say nothing about the immense losses and waste in experimenting. But the company can take contracts—"lose money"—and make it back in money through rental.

Point 4. Mr. Pullman offered to allow the employees the privilege of inspecting his books.

This is true, but the employees had no need to consult his books. There may have been a few who did not believe he lost money on certain contracts, but the majority of them accepted his statement as correct. There were those, however, who believed that in some way or other the books were "doctored" to suit the Company's side of the question, and still others that there was a double set of books kept by the company which would make it impossible to get at the facts in the case. While this may not be true, still it indicates the suspicious condition of mind engendered by the Company's past treatment of its employees. And further, with such a complicated and intricate system of bookkeeping as that of the Pullman Company, how could working-men be expected to arrive at conclusions therefrom?

Point 5. In his final statement Mr. Pullman re-
fers to the question of arbitration, and very ingeni-
ously evades the whole question at issue. He says:

"How could I, as president of the Pullman company, consent to agree that if any body of men not
concerned with the interests of the company's share-
holders should as arbitrators, for any reasons seem-
ing good to them, so decree, I would open the shops,
employ workmen at wages greater than their work
could be sold for and continue this ruinous policy
indefinitely or be accused of a breach of faith? Who
will deny that such a question is plainly not a subject of arbitration? Is it not, then, unreasonable
that the company should be asked to arbitrate whether
or not it should submit such a question to arbitration?"

Now, it was never asked of Mr. Pullman that he
consent to arbitration with the condition attached that
he open his shops and employ his men at wages
greater than their work could be sold for. Nor was
he asked to continue his ruinous policy indefinitely.
When approached by the Committee of the Common Council, all that was asked of him was arbitration on the question as to whether or not there was
anything to arbitrate. If his position was right,
then he had nothing to fear. It is absurd to attempt
to treat the relation between a giant corporation and
its army of organized workmen quite on the old
simple footing of one employer and his one hired
man. Arbitration alone can settle these difficulties.
I submit if here is not a basis of arbitration: 1.
Less cut in wages. 2. Reduction of rents. 3.
Equalization of wages. 4. Reform of abuses practiced in the shops.

CHAPTER VII.

CUTTING WAGES.

Let the general public remember one thing which has caused the Pullman employees to stand in a wrong light before the world. They are quoted as wanting the wages of '93 for work done at a loss. When the employees agreed to ask for the wages of '93 they did what a great many people do, they intended to ask for a certain thing and failing in that t o compromise on what they really did want. They felt their cause was just and if they failed to get the restoration of the scale of 1893, they expected that the Company would agree to lessen the severity of the cut in wages (say to make it about 25 per cent, instead of 33 1-2 per cent), and then to reduce their rents, equalize their wages, and change the innumerable petty abuses to which they were being subjected in the shops. Mr. Pullman, however, was too sharp for them, and instead of generously and openly deciding to do what every just person agrees ought to have been done, he found it very convenient to take the men at their word and, without any compromise, evade the main issue under the specious plea of not being able to pay wages of '93 on the basis of losing contracts.

It is generally agreed that the maximum average wage paid at the time of the strike was $1.85. As to the lowest wages, it is difficult to average. The wages are paid every two weeks. Two checks are given to each employee—one a rent check, the other a pay check. Wages are paid at the bank. When they go to the bank to receive their two weeks' pay the half month's rent is taken out, and the pay check cashed. The scenes enacted at the bank during last winter were pitiable. Not only was the current rent urgently demanded, but back rent was asked for under circumstances in many cases entirely uncalled for. After deducting rent the men invariably had only from one to six dollars or so on which to live for two weeks. One man has a pay check in his possession of *two* cents after paying rent. He has never cashed it, preferring to keep it as a memento. He has it framed. Another I saw the other day, for *seven* cents. It was dated September, '93. The man had worked as a skilled mechanic at ten hours a day for twelve days, and earned $9.07. He keeps a widowed mother, and pays the rent, the house being in his name. His half month's rent amounted to $9.00. The seven cents was his, but he has never claimed it. Another employee had 47 cents coming to him on his pay check, and then was asked if he would not apply that on his back rent. He was indignant. He replied: "If Mr. Pullman needs that 47 cents worse than I do, let him have it." He left it.

Many employees took advantage of the present law governing wages, and retained a part and sometimes all their rent money to sustain their families. Thus it was that the employees fell in arrears in rent to the extent of $70,000.

The average cut in wages was 33 1-3 per cent; in some cases it was as much as 40 per cent, and in many was fifty per cent. These cuts in wages without corresponding reduction in rents were very severe, and largely produced the dissatisfaction which resulted in the strike.

As for those who had always earned good wages and were living in the better class of houses, these cuts bore down upon them with increasing severity. One man, an expert in certain kinds of work, not necessary to mention, as it might injure him, was cut from thirty-five cents an hour to twenty-three cents, and was about to be cut lower. These wages, even when cut, were not so bad, but the great trouble in so many cases was they could not put in full time. This man, all through the winter, earned just barely enough each pay day to meet his rent. His wife, taking in boarders and roomers, was thus able to keep the wolf from the door. A first-class mechanic worked ten hours a day for two weeks and then only earned $9.90. Laborers in the fall and winter earned nine cents an hour shifting lumber.

In this whole question of wages the public must bear in mind that the wage difficulty was not the whole trouble. Other things being equal, the men could have borne with more grace the reduction of wages. But there was personal abuse and tyrannical dealing in the shops, no reduction of rents, the loss of time, and a hundred minor abuses inherent in the system, that make the question of wages in Pullman different to that found in any other place. There is but one town of Pullman in America, and that is *sui generis*.

While all the employees were cut in wages, many were still able to live, gentlemen as they are, who on principle, were willing to bear almost anything rather than complain. A goodly number had no particular complaint at all, but while opposed to the strike, they were in hearty sympathy with those upon whom the burden of the cut was most severe. The cuts seemed to fall unequally on different classes of employees, the scale was changed so often that the men were in a constant condition of wonderment as to what would be the next move. The worst feature was that while the most of the work was done by piece work rather than time work, they did not have the opportunity to put in full time. For two or three months in the winter the hours of labor were seven hours a day. Later, as work increased, the time in· creased to ten hours per day. The employees complained bitterly of their loss of time, all through the winter. I heard it on every side. In a large establishment like the Pullman Shops there must necessa-

rily be a large force of foremen, under foremen, sub-
bosses, as well as heads of departments and higher
officials. Instead of decreasing these foremen and
under bosses, while cutting wages, these sub-bosses
and inspectors were increased to such an extent as
to make it positively unbearable in certain departments.

The employees were cut on an average of 33 1-2
per cent in their wages, many of them 40 per cent
and not a few 50 per cent. Trimmers were compelled
to work on a car by contract so low, that after the
wages was worked out, it would take three to five days
to finish the car, and not one cent allowed to them
thereon. First-class mechanics would work ten
hours a day for two weeks and receive $9 90. La-
borers were known to labor for nine cents an hour
for ten hours' work, and earn the glorious sum of
ninety cents per day. Inspectors or sub-bosses were
placed over little gangs of men, to see that the same
quality of work was squeezed out of the already cruelly
reduced employees, as they had always been doing.
It was, therefore, not surprising in many cases that
the wages were so low that with the high rents they
could not live.

Let me illustrate by the case of a mechanic employed in the iron department He works on a certain machine.

He earned $1.40 per day. If he has full time
(which he has not) he earns $36.40 in one month.

We will say that he is a married man and occupies a flat of five rooms, for which he pays $14.50 per month. This leaves him $21.90 to clothe, feed and otherwise provide for his family, or about eighty-four cents per day. He can get another flat for $12.50, in a house having four flats to the building, on another street. He can live in the tenement blocks for $9.00 or $7.00. But what man who desires to bring up his family aright desires to live there?

You can make the same calculation upon the basis of $1.85, which all agree was the average wages paid at the time of the strike. Out of that $1.85 per day you must deduct rent and water rate, on the basis of $18.50 plus 71 cents, $17.00 plus 71 cents, $14.50 plus 50 cents, $12.50 plus 50 cents, $6.50 plus 50 cents, $8.60 plus 50 cents, brick yards $8.00. Before drawing conclusions, read chapter on rents, and see what your intelligent American mechanic gets in return for the above rents, and which kind of rent he will be most likely to come under.

One man, a common laborer with a family to support, said he received for the days he was given work forty-nine cents a day. His rent for the month, including water rates, was $8.21. There was left out of his pay check less than $3 with which to support his family two weeks.

One of the blacksmiths who was at the works for years says he, when at work, earned forty-five cents in six hours. When the Pullman Company's ultima-

tum was given that the strikers must go to work at the
reduced rates or leave Pullman, he declared that he
would leave, because if he had to starve he wouldn't
starve and wear out his clothes at the same time at
Pullman's anvil.   He and his companions, he said,
were among the first to get out.

Another man, a few days before the strike, got a pay
check for his month's labor which came forty-five
cents short of balancing his rent account.   A bill for
its balance was made out and the collector was sent
with it to his house for payment. What this man was
going to live on until his next pay check and next
month's rent were due, he didn't know, and he did not
require much persuasion to quit.

The blacksmiths, who formerly made from $4 a day
upwards, say that at the time they went on strike,
after three cuts in their wages within six weeks, they
could not average more than $1 a day.   One of
them, a man who is counted one of the best opera-
tors in the shop, was only able to make $1.03 in
three days.

Carvers, who are a very high grade of skilled arti-
sans and who generally receive high wages, had been,
at the time of the strike, cut down until they received
only twenty-five cents an hour.

Stripers, another high grade of workmen, got twenty
cents an hour, while painters got only nineteen cents.
A part of the winter they were only permitted to
work seven hours.

It seems that these cuts were worse in some departments than in others; and even in the same departments there would be a strange lack of equalization.

I will quote here a letter written by Miss Jennie Curtiss, an employee of the Company, which will give, in her own language, a description of the Company's treatment of the employees in the women's department. I have read this letter to a young woman, an employee in the "New Work" department, who is very conservative and reliable, and well qualified to testify on these points. She corroborates everything written herein:

"Being an employee of the Pullman Company for the past five years, I can truthfully state the following. There are two sewing rooms in the Pullman works; one is where all the new work is done, such as new carpets, window curtains, silk, satin, velvet, and plush draperies made for parlor, dining and chair cars only. We also sew the plush and tapestry with which the seats and backs of the sleepers are upholstered, and make all the sheets, pillow-slips, table-cloths, towels, napkins and linen of all descriptions used in the dining cars and sleepers. We also make all kinds of berth curtains.

"Then there is the Repair shop sewing room, where all of the repairing is done. I have worked in both departments, three years and a half in the new sewing room, and one year and a half in the Repair shop sewing rooms. The work in these sewing rooms is made mostly piece work and some day work. I will state some of our prices.

1893................carpet, 90 cents a section.
1894................carpet, 20 cents a section.

"It is true we were making these carpets (under the reduction) by machine, that is about half of them, and the other half of them had to be finished by hand, and the machine sewing did not save ten per cent of the work, and I have known girls that made these carpets by machine at twenty cents a section, to only make five cents an hour. These carpets are cut and made in sections. The carpet is all in one, but it is cut in such odd shapes and slashes made to fit the cars that from one cut to the other we call a section. These carpets are large and small, they run from four to nine sections; therefore a nine section carpet that we received ninety cents a section for in 1893, would be $8.10; in 1894 at twenty cents a section, only $1.80. There have been a great many mistakes made about the prices of these carpets in the statements of the papers, and that is why I have tried to explain as much as possible in regard to them.

1893	A three window drapery.	$1.50
1894	" " " "	80
1893	A two window drapery	1.25
1894	" " " "	48
1893	A one window drapery	1.00
1894	" " " "	45
1893	1 enclosed section curtain	35
1894	" " " "	15
1893	1 mattress tick, folding (37 1-2),	40
1894	1 " " "	18
1893	1 " " single (27),	25
1894	1 " " "	10

"These prices are in the Repair shop sewing room, in which place I worked last. They get the same price for the same work in the new room, but the prices on the linen and several other things I can not give. There are numerous other kinds of work we make for the cars, which would take too much time and space to mention, which has all been cut from time to time to the very lowest standard. For four years we were allowed to make $2.25 a day at the prices of 1893, which was very good wages for a girl, but which we well earned, as it was very tedious and confining, and long hours. At the time the shops closed on account of the strike, I was earning on an average eighty cents a day, at the prices of 1894. It was very hard to have to work for such small wages as that, which would afford a person a mere existence. But the tyrannical and abusive treatment we received from our forewoman made our daily cares so much harder to bear. She was a woman who had sewed and lived among us for years, one, you would think, who would have some compassion on us when she was put in a position to do so. When she was put over us by the superintendent as our forewoman, she seemed to delight in showing her power in hurting the girls in every possible way. At times her conduct was almost unbearable. She was so abusive to certain girls that she disliked, that they could not stand it, and would take their time and leave, who would otherwise have been working there to-day. If she could make you do a piece of work for twenty-five cents less than the regular price, she would do so every time. In fact she cut a great deal of work down *herself*. I have had many a dispute with her myself about cutting down our prices just to get the work done cheaper, thinking she would stand in better with the Company. She was getting $2.25 a day and she did not care how much we girls made, whether we made enough to live on or not, just so long as she could figure to save a few dollars for the Company. When a girl was sick and asked to go home during the day, she would tell them to their face they were not sick, the cars had to be got out, and they could not go home. She also had a few favorites in the room, to whom she gave all the best work, that they could make the most money on. We would complain of her to the foreman and general foreman, but they all upheld her, and if you were not willing to take her abuse you could go. There is now lying in Mr. Wickes' office in Chicago a petition signed by fifteen girls in the sewing room, requesting her removal. There are only eighteen girls working under her. No doubt she will remain in the employ of the Pullman Company, as that is just the kind of people they want at the heads of their departments—one who will help grind down their laborers. My father worked for the Pullman Company for *ten* years. Last summer he was sick for three months, and in September he died. At the time of his death we owed the Pullman Company about sixty dollars for rent. I was working at the time and they told me I would have to pay that rent, give what I could every pay-day, until it was paid. I did not say I would not pay, but thought rather than be thrown out of work I would pay it. Many a time I have drawn nine and ten dollars for two weeks' work, paid seven dollars for my board and given the Company the remaining two or three dollars on the rent, and I still owe them fifteen dollars. Sometimes when I could not possibly give them anything, I would receive slurs and insults from the clerks in the bank, because Mr. Pullman would not give me enough in return for my hard labor to pay the rent for one of his houses and live.

JENNIE CURTISS."

Here is another letter, written by an employee in the freight department. Some pitiable tales are told by the freight-car builders, concerning their hardships during the past winter. I have the man's name and address, but will not use it, for fear of retaliation:

"Pullman, Ill., July 22, '94.

REV. W. H. CARWARDINE.

DEAR SIR:—I will try and give you a few facts. I am a freight-car builder, have worked for the Pullman Co. since the 10th of January, 1892, and I don't think we asked too much when we asked our wages restored to what they were in 1893, as we did not make any more than a fair living at that time. The highest pay that I made for two weeks in 1893 was $34.72, and I can truly say that my wages for the year did not exceed $1.80 per pay. Up to the beginning of the strike, I had run in debt about one hundred dollars; one half of this for rent, the rest for groceries and meat. I have reported for work every day that the shops were open for work, up till the strike began, and never missed even one hour, except when I moved my family here. I have a wife and four children, and it was for them that I struck, as I think that when a man is sober and steady, and has a saving wife, one who is willing to help along, and after working two and a half years for a company he finds himself in debt for a common living, something must be wrong. Some folks have said that we should have been satisfied. So we would have been, if we had been assured that this cut of fifty per cent was only temporary, and the Company had done the fair thing on the rent at the same time. But no! I was told just before the strike by one of the foremen that the Company had work for six months, and if we had kept on the Company would have owned us by that time. So with a prospect of working an indefinite length of time at these prices and under an *overbearing* and *profane* foreman, we struck and will stay out until the battle is fairly won, or we have to step out for good, and I believe if we do have to move out, the Pullman Company will rue the day, because I never saw a better class of mechanics than there are in Pullman to-day, and I never lived in a more orderly town in my life, and I don't believe there would have been one single dollar's worth of property destroyed in this town if the Company hadn't gone to the expense that they have, as well as the city and state. I don't think that George M. Pullman is as well acquainted with his children as he pretends to be, or he would have known that there was not one single anarchist in his whole family. Leaving you to use any part of this, or all if you wish, I remain,

Very respectfully yours."

"P. S. I was born in the United States, as were my parents before me and as were their parents before them."

The following statement will give some definite idea to the general reader as to the reduction of wages in the Freight Department:

"Pullman, July 23, 1894.

REV. W. H. CARWARDINE.

DEAR SIR:—I have been employed as car-builder in the freight department of the Pullman Palace Car Company for the past twelve years. The best wages that I ever averaged as car-builder was $2.10 per day, and when the strike began my wages averaged seventy cents per day. I have paid $11.57 per month rent for the past eight years. The treatment we have received from the foreman of the Company has been worse than the slaves ever received in the south.

"I shall give you some prices paid. These figures I take from a ledger secured from the general time-keeper from the freight shops.

Lot 1515............................Oct., 1888
Car-builder.............................$13.00
Truck builder..............................90
Truck labor................................31
Hanging brakes...........................1.20
Delivery forgings.........................1.05
Delivery lumber............................88
Framing ... .40

Total....................$17.74

"The same car with latest improvements, in November, 1893.

Car-builder..............................$7.00
Truck   " 60
Truck labor................................09
Hanging brakes............................65
Delivery forgings..........................35
Delivery lumber............................21
Framing....................................12

Total....................$9.02

Average wages in 1888 ....$2.26
Average "   " 1893....................$1.03

"I shall show figures of the car that we struck on, the Wickes Refrigerator, in 1889.

Car-builders............................$36.00
Truck   " 90
Truck labor................................32
Hanging brakes...........................1.20
Delivery forgings........................1.31
Delivery lumber..........................1.46
Framing....................................85

Total....................$42.04

"The same car, 1894, with the latest improvements.

Car builder	$19.50
Truck "	60
Truck labor	10
Hanging brakes	60
Delivery forgings	56
Delivery lumber	64
Framing	26

Total $22.26

Reduction of	$19 78
Average of wages 1889	$2.00 per day
Average " " 1894	91 per day

Respectfully."

The following table will indicate the reductions in the upholsterers' department. The list of reductions here used throughout the chapter, are taken from the statement of the Strikers' Central Committee in their report to the A. R. U. Convention. They claim that they are taken from the official books of the Company. I have submitted them for corroboration to a gentleman who has been for many years a trusted employee of the Company, who is an entirely disinterested party and is in a position to know, and he says that they are correct:

	1893.	1894.
Tufted head rests, with springs................	$ .85	$ .41
Tufted head rests, without springs..............	.65	.41
Spring-edge backs........	.67	.48½
Spring-edge seats, tufted......................	1.10	.79
Spring-edge seats, plain......................	.90	.65
Aisle ends......................	.70	.47
Wall ends......................................	.65	.47
Scroll ends....................................	1.25	.70
Mann boudoir seat, tufted.....................	3.00	1.70
Mann boudoir seat, plain.....................	2.75	1.51
Mann boudoir back............................	4.00	2.85
Dining car plush seats........................	.37	.34
Dining car leather seats......................	.43¼	.34
Dining car plush back.........................	.85	.54
Dining car leather back.......................	.95	.54
Drawing-room sofa seats......................	3.50	2.40
Smoking room sofa seats......................	3.50	2.75
Extra long sofa seats.........................	4.00	2.75
Round-end sofa seats.........................	2.75	2.10
Drawing-room sofa backs, plain...............	.60	.39
Drawing-room sofa backs, tufted..............	2.00	1.23
Smoking-room sofa backs, double..............	4.00	2.88
Smoking-room sofa backs, single..............	2.00	1.28
Sofa panels, tufted...........................	.60	.42
Sofa panels, with arms........................	.75	.42
Plush panels, per car.........................	1.02	.79
Sofa rolls....................................	1.40	.90
Large car chairs....	5.75	4.00
Detroit chairs................................	5.50	3.60
Wicker chair, square..........................	4.50	3.20
Wicker chair, round..........................	4.50	2.90
Wicker chair, No. 369........................	3.00	1.75
Wicker chair, No. 1,036......................	1.00	.70
Wicker sofa..................................	10.00	5.00
Cutting carpets, dining car....................	2.00	.90
Cutting carpets, sleeping car..................	2.00	1.10
Cutting carpets, Wilton.......................	2.50	1.50
Laying carpet and oil cloth....................	1.25	.80
Mattresses, new folding.......................	.30	.20
Mattresses, double...........................	.25	.15
Mattresses, smoking-room.....................	.40	.22
Mattresses, old single........................	.20	.15
Mattresses, tourist...........................	.23	.15
Loose cushions...............................	.25	.20
Spring-edge seats, day coaches................	.79	.62
Hard-edge seats, day coaches.................	.43	.35
Backs, day coaches	.30	.27
Day work....................................	2.75	1.90
Day work....................................	2.50	1.90
Day work....................................	2.25	1 80
Day work....................................	2.00	1.50
Day work, laborers...........................	1.50	1.30

Among the painters the following table will give some idea as to their reductions:

	1893.	1894.
Ornamental painters	$ 2.75	$ 2.30
Ornamental painters...............................	2.50	2.30
Hardwood finishers................................	2.35	2.00
Hardwood finishers........................	2.30	1.75
Rubbers...	2.20	1.50

Piece work prices have been so reduced that the men can with the utmost difficulty make their day rate. The ornamentation of a Pullman sleeper was reduced from $40 to $25.30, rubbing rough stuff from $22 to $15, and all other work in the same proportion. It must be borne in mind that the painters in Chicago have by their recent strike secured for themselves thirty-five cents an hour for eight hours' work until June 15, and 32 1-2 cents an hour thereafter. The men in Pullman have extraordinary skill, but are paid at the rate of twenty-three cents an hour, a difference to-day of twelve cents. In other words, the Chicago brotherhood men are getting nearly fifty-two per cent more than the members of the American Railway Union. If it be asked why the men do not leave Pullman, it can only be answered that many of them have already, and that more will follow. But they demand justice where they are.

The machinists (Bolt Headers' Dept.) are asking for the same scale of wages as paid by the Chicago Forge and Bolt Company for precisely the same work. The differences are startling, the Pullman men since the cutting, for example, getting only six and one-fourth cents a hundred for three-quarter bolts, while the Chicago concern is paying eleven and three-fourth cents. The reduction in this department amounts to nearly fifty per cent. The threaders, millwrights, punch handlers, drill hands, and tool-makers ask for the wages of 1893. These last, who make tools, are cut in some cases to $1 75 a day, from $2.75 paid last December. In addition, the superintendent of this department is a bookkeeper, merely, and has frequently admitted that he knows nothing whatever about machinery or the requirements of the work.

Among the Foundrymen, the brass molders have been cut from twenty to twenty-five cents a day, and the laborers and furnace men twenty cents. The brass finishers lost from twenty-five to fifty cents a day. The molders in the wheel shop were cut five cents a wheel, amounting to $1 and $1.20 a day, while the helpers have fifty cents a day less and the laborers ten to thirty-five cents. In the last year the men in this department have only been given twenty-eight days' actual employment. The machine department men were reduced twenty-five cents a day. The iron foundrymen who do piece work were reduced from forty to seventy-five cents for ten hours' work, the day workmen forty cents, coremakers from twenty to eighty cents, men in the chipping room twenty to seventy-five cents, and the yardmen twenty cents.

The blacksmiths suffered a cut between thirty and fifty per cent. Smiths making from $3.50 to $4.00 a day were cut down to between $1.50 and $2.50, the helpers suffering accordingly.

Among the employees of the Pullman Company there are a number of young women working in the carpet department, the new linen-room, the linen repair room, the glass-embossing department, and the laundry. Before May, 1893, the various departments were all paid at the rate of twenty-two and one-half cents an hour. The cut reduced this to ten cents an hour, a scaling down of sixty-eight per cent.

Many girls providing for invalid mothers or small sisters or brothers have been able to make but six cents an hour. The Illinois statutes compel an eight-hour day for women.

The special grievance of the wood-machine hands seemed to lie in their opposition to piece work. They have suffered in some instances a cut of forty per cent, and in no case has it fallen below thirty-three and one-third per cent. Some reductions are appalling. Work on parlor cars formerly worth $35 went down to $5, and on day coaches from $6 to $1.75.

The following are the reductions made in the Street Cars department since May 1st, 1893:—

Body Builders, Inside Finishers and Trimmers, from $3 per day to $2 per day. Cabinet makers were cut fifty per cent, Wood machinists from $2.75 and $2.25 per day to $2.40 and $1.60 per day. Blacksmiths were cut sixty per cent. Iron Machinists were cut eighty-five per cent. In this shop if a man made a complaint the foreman discharged him, telling him that he would bring one of his own countrymen over, who would do as much work as any six Americans. The shop laborers were cut from $1.50 to $1 30 per day. Painters were cut from $3.00 per day to $2.10. Stripers and ornamenters cut about sixty per cent. This is a sample of prices for a standard closed car

	1892.	1893.	1894.
Body	$ 41.00	$ 33 50	$ 25.00
Inside finish	30.00	27.00	22.00
Trimming	....	17.00	12.00

In view of these extensive and repeated cuttings of wages, it is no wonder that sometimes pay checks showed laborers, rated at $1.35 per day, often get-

ting but ninety-one cents for seven hours' work, and
finishers or trimmers making but $13.70 or even $6.57
for two weeks' work, out of which, by the terms of
the leases, the rents had to be deducted. As I have
said before, there were any number of cases contin-
ually, where the pay check amounted to less than five
dollars, and in some instances but a few cents left
after paying the rent.

Imagine how a workman must feel after laboring
two weeks, to step up to the bank, and have either
two cents, seven cents, eight cents, or forty-seven cents
handed to him to keep his family on for the following two weeks. Not much "mutual recognition" in
that!

In connection with the cutting of wages it must
be remembered that the failure to equalize wages produced great injustice and many hardships among the
employees. I have it on good authority that after the
Annual Meeting of last year the Company decided
upon a general policy of reorganization throughout
the whole shops. In view of this, work was slackened
in all departments, no new work was taken, the employees were laid off until, along in September, I was
told by the manager that there were not more than
900 to 1,200 men on the list. I understand that the
"general policy" adopted was to take advantage of the
"hard times," and open up later with a view to cutting wages. It was supposed that the employees, being in debt to the Company in rent, would be glad of

work, and accept "cuts" with better grace than if the shops had not been practically shut down for two or three months. I believe Mr. Pullman and Mr. Wickes were desirous of putting this policy into force gradually and evenly, and I have reason to know that Mr. Pullman did not wish the men to be crowded more than they were willing to endure. His orders were, "Go slow." His managers "drove fast." Driven to desperation by repeated slashings and cuttings of the managerial whips, the employees took° the bit in their teeth, and upset the coach in the ditch. Mr. Pullman, absent half of his time from the city, scarcely coming to the town more than five or six times during the winter, knew nothing about the true state of affairs. Statements from every department, weekly and so forth, were sent to him, but before reaching him there is no doubt that they were colored with such a roseate hue that he naturally believed all was well. What an easy thing for him to drop down unexpectedly, post himself on the real state of affairs, and act accordingly! For failure to do that, I hold that he is responsible for the present state of affairs.

A word as to equalization. First of all, when the wages of the employees were cut, why did he not cut the salaries of the officials, the clerical force, the heads of departments, the foremen, inspectors, etc.? True, some of the foremen, when they were taken back to work last fall, did so at less pay than when they went out, but they were the only ones, and that was not a "cut" similar to that received by the employees later on.

Then, again, here is what I mean by equalization. Blacksmith laborers, required to do the hardest kind of work, were reduced from $1.50 to $1.30 per day. Now, on the Passenger Car department a laborer whose work was comparatively light and easy, was cut just the same, $1.50 to $1.30. I contend, in justice, that the blacksmith's laborer ought to have been cut *less* than the other laborer.

Again, cabinet-makers and upholsterers were cut about the same, say from $2.75 to $1.85; some as low as $1.55 to $1.50 day rate. Now, a cabinet-maker should not be cut as low as an upholsterer, for the cabinet-maker has to provide himself with a kit of tools valued from $75.00 to $100.00, with the danger of loss by breakage, etc., besides years of preparation for his special work. While the upholsterer's work is important and requires skilled labor, yet it is not as high grade work as the cabinet-maker's. Yet they are cut the same, without regard to skill, etc. Even if they are on piece work, they are not allowed to make more than day rate. In some cases they were both cut so low that they could not even make day rate. Then, again, it must be remembered that in all departments through the shops the scale of wages paid, even in 1893, was below the Union scale in vogue throughout Chicago and elsewhere. During the past year in Pullman, skilled mechanics could not make as much as day laborers made in 1893, with a few exceptions.

Another case in point. A fireman employed in heating the great boilers of the Corliss engine, hard and laborious employment, works the first two weeks of the month for eighty-six hours per week, and the next two weeks for one hundred and twenty-six hours per week, seven days in the week. He thus labors 428 hours per month or about sixteen hours per day, and receives therefrom $40.00 per month pay.

Or again, an employee in the iron machine shop is given a job consisting of fifty pieces of iron, each with four holes, which are to be squared and trimmed. It takes him just one hour to finish one piece, and according to the scale given to him by the under-foreman, he will receive four and one-half cents per piece; four and one-half cents for one hour's work, and he a good mechanic, capable of earning $3.00 per day. He appeals to the superintendent, a good man, a practical man; he sees the injustice of the case, agrees to have it remedied, and when the man was paid, he found he had been allowed twenty cents for them instead of four and one-half cents. Now, this man was fortunate in getting justice, but all over the shops men were imposed upon and mistreated in this way, who got no redress.

Mr. Pullman says "nothing to arbitrate." I appeal to the public if there was not "something to arbitrate" here—less reductions, and equalization of wages.

In concluding this chapter, I would add that two-thirds of the abuses practiced in the shops arose over this unmerciful cutting of wages. It seemed to be the policy from high official down to sub-boss, to see how often and how much they could "cut" their men. Employees who occupied positions of influence, were seemingly discharged because they did not "cut" to suit those over them; the imported gentlemen who took the places of those vacated, in order to sustain their reputation for reducing expenses, must necessarily "cut" and grind those beneath them. Apparently when gentlemen who had been in the employ of the Company seven, eleven and twenty years, all capable and practical men, of irreproachable character, had pressure brought to bear on them to resign, and their places filled with men, not practical, some not as irreproachable in character as they might be, but whose sole claim to position was that they would not hesitate to put the screws on the already reduced employees, then it seems to me that the Pullman Company has forgotten about its "mutual recognition" theory, and *prefers* to have just such as these latter at the head of the affairs. And these are the gentlemen who at the first alarm of violence cry to the government for military protection, fill the town on the slightest provocation with the police, and who themselves are so afraid of their mortal existence that they move about armed to the teeth, and in quick communication with the militia. *O tempora! O mores!*

Let the reader place beside this sad picture that other one that men love so well to contemplate, the Pullman Palace Car Company, $27,000,000 surplus. Capitalization of $30,000,000. Two per cent quarterly dividend of $600,000 in three months!

CHAPTER VIII.

When Mr. Pullman said that he had "nothing to arbitrate" he evidently must have forgotten for the time being the high rents and exorbitant, prices demanded for water and gas in his "model town." Mr. Pullman in his final statement says:

"A few words are pertinent as to some industriously spread charges against the Company. One of these charges is that rents are exorbitant, and it is implied that the Pullman employees have no choice but to submit. The answer is simple: The average rental of tenements at Pullman is at the rate of $3 per room per month, and the renting of houses at Pullman has no relation to the work in the shops. Employees may, and very many do, own or rent their houses outside of the town, and the buildings and business places in the town are rented to employees or to others, in competition with the neighboring properties. In short, the renting business of the Pullman Company is governed by the same conditions which govern any other large owner of real estate, except that the company itself does directly some things which in Chicago are assumed by the city. If, therefore, it is not admitted that the rents of any landlord are to be fixed. by arbitration and that those of the adjoining towns of Kensington and Roseland should also be so fixed, it can hardly be

asked that the Pullman Company alone should
abandon the ordinary rules which govern persons in
that relation."

Let us examine this carefully. He says that $3.00
per room is the average rental. According to page
fifty-one of Mr. Duane Doty's book on the Town of
Pullman, there are 1,855 tenements in Pullman. A
few have been added, however, since the publication
of Mr. Doty's book. Averaging five rooms to a house,
that would make it $3.71 per room. But it must be
remembered that at least one-half the tenements are
now empty, and about one-third of them have always
been empty. Last year, on account of the World's
Fair, was about the only year in the history of the
town when the houses were all practically occupied.
If we should base an average on the actual rents paid
and the actual number of houses occupied, we would
find a much higher rental than $3 00 per 100m. But
look at facts, not averages. I occupied a flat of four
rooms on Watt Ave., and paid $14.50 rent; at $3.00
per room, I lost $2.50 per month. I next rented a
five room cottage on Morse Ave., for $17.50; at $3.00
per room, lost $2.50 per month. I am now renting
a five room cottage on same street, but a better loca-
tion, for $18.50; at $3.00 per room, I am losing $3.50
per month.

In Frank Leslie's *Illustrated Weekly*, published in
New York, July 26, '94, Mr. John T. Bramhall truthfully says:

"I had read that the rents of houses here range from $5 to $50 per month, the average being $14; but there are hundreds of tenements ranging from $6 to $9 per month. These rents are considerably less than for similar tenements anywhere else in Chicago.

"The above was written several years ago, when rents were higher than they are now. Briefly this is what I found, as verified by the rent receipts, the odd cents standing for the water rate: Flat, seven rooms and bath, $28.96; the same in other Chicago suburbs, $18 to $20. Flat, five rooms, $15.60; flat, four rooms, $14.71; apartments in "block," a three story tenement building in the middle of a square, containing from seventeen to fifty-four families— three rooms, $9.10; two rooms, $7.60."

I quote from Mr. Doty's book, written in the interest of the company: "Single five room cottages rent from $16 to $19 per month, while single houses of from six to nine rooms vary from $22 to $10 per month." While these are cottages, it must be remembered that they are not detached, but are built side by side with other brick houses in rows. I pay $18.50 for a five room cottage and seventy-one cents for water, with the use of only one faucet, and no bath-room. Four and five room apartments in two-story flats rent from $14 to $15 per month, plus the water at 60 to 71 cents per month. Four room apartments on the first, second and third floors of three-story flats rent from $11 to $13.50 per month, plus the water at sixty cents per month.

In the large tenement blocks, where from 300 to 500 people live under one roof, you can get two rooms on third floor in the rear for $6.50 plus sixty cents for water, or four rooms for $8.50 plus sixty cents for water. On the second floor of same building you pay $8.50, plus sixty cents, for three rooms. In the brick yards, a place not fit for any decent human being to live in, you can rent a three room cottage for $8.00. The water is free; one outdoor faucet for every four houses. There are some very high-priced houses in town. Taking all cottages, tenements and flats together, I should judge that the average rental would be more likely to be $18.00 than $14.00.

The town of Pullman is estimated to be worth $10,000,000. Everything pays rent. The "Green-stone Church," as I have already intimated, pays $1,200, the Methodist Church, in the Casino building, pays nearly $500. The Y. M. C. A. pays $180 per year. The 1,800 dwellings pay $325,-000 or more. The market, the arcade, and the stores bring in a good rental besides.

Mr. Pullman further says that "the renting of houses in Pullman has no relation to the work in the shops." Now, what does he mean? Was not the town built principally to rent to the employees? That is the very theory upon which it is established. The employees are positively expected to live in Pullman. Last winter, when work was slack, the shops picked up, and the men were re-employed. The orders then were, as told me by the manager himself, first to take on men renting in Pullman, second those who own

their own homes in adjoining towns, and third those
who do not rent in Pullman or own homes elsewhere.
That was right. The renters should have first choice.
When the shops were filled up, and the houses well
taken, then employees could be free to live elsewhere.
Sometimes there are certain mechanics whom the
Company are compelled to have; they can live where
they please. If necessary, I can give names of men
who have told me that they were urged and re-urged
to move to Pullman, or be "laid off." The employees,
as a rule, are expected to rent the Company's houses.
There are many exceptions, it is true, but this is the
unwritten if not the written law of the Company. I
know many men who would prefer not to live here,
but are practically expected to. If the employees
should all move out of town some fine morning when
work is in full blast, the Company would soon testify to its position on that point.

Mr. Pullman further states in regard to rent that
he charges rents in Pullman in competition with
rents in adjoining towns. Here is a letter written
by a Kensington real estate dealer to the *Chicago
Times* on this question. I quote:

"Kensington, Ill., July 17.—GEORGE M. PULLMAN,
ESQ., Long Branch, N. J.—Sir: In the publishment
of a recent interview with you it is stated that your
renting department charges rents in Pullman in competition with rents in the adjoining towns of Kensington, Roseland, and Gano. If you sincerely
believe this to be true, it would be well for you to
personally investigate, as with my six years' experi-

ence in the renting business in the said towns of Kensington, Roseland, and Gano, I know it to be a positive fact that flats and cottages containing parlor, dining-room, two bedrooms and kitchen, with use of water and yard, have been and are rented for $10 and $12, for which similar accommodations you charge $16 and $18 at least.

"My statement, undoubtedly, will be verified at any time by the other renting agents of this district.

"Respectfully,   CORNELIUS G. BOON,
            Real estate and renting agent."

There is no question whatever but that better flats and cottages, with pretty garden, and bath-rooms, can be hired at the neighboring towns of Roseland and Kensington at fully twenty per cent less.

The water tax has always been a burden upon the people. Bought under contract for four cents per 1,000 gallons, it was retailed to the tenants for ten cents per 1,000 gallons. The rates to the tenants individually are given above. Since Mayor Hopkins took office the price to the town of Pullman has been increased, and now this company is said to be making little if anything on the water. As to the gas, it is a well known fact that we all pay $2.25 per thousand feet, while in Chicago it is sold for $1.25 and $1.00.

A few interesting details might be added concerning the town. A recent table of the nativity of the wage-earners at Pullman shows the following:

American	1,796	Dutch	753
Scandinavian	1,422	Irish	402
German	824	Latin	170
British and Canadian	796	All others	161

6,324

The town controls 3,500 acres of land, formerly swamp land, in its original native state worth probably not over $15·00 per acre. About one hundred acres is covered with dwellings and other buildings, valued at about $5,000,000, and two hundred more given up to factories, foundry, shops, steel mills, etc., equaling no doubt about $11,000,000, all told. It is a fact that has been stated repeatedly without denial that this vast property only brings into the city of Chicago a pittance of $15,000.00 annually by taxes, less than one-tenth of one per cent of its estimated value. It is assessed apparently per acre rather than by lot. What is the matter with the assessor?

Mr. Pullman objects to the arbitration of his rents and compares himself and company to the ordinary real estate dealer. This is not a fair comparison. The Pullman Palace Car Company is so established that all its interests are clearly related one to another. The town of Pullman and the shops are inseparable. They are intimately related to each other. The demand of the men for reduction of rents is reasonable and ought to be heeded; above all, when they are expected to live in his houses, he should be willing while cutting their income, to reduce their expenses.

CHAPTER IX.

In this chapter we deal with one of the vital causes of the Pullman Strike. Shop abuses and mismanagement have had no little to do with the present condition of affairs. Mr. Pullman spent much money in building his ideal city, but laid it out in accordance with the feudal system, everything belonging to the lord of the manor. It was an experiment, on American soil. Mr. Pullman thought he would make a success of it. But it has practically failed.

He got the best class of workmen to be found, and paid the highest wages. They earned them, for they were experts; his laboring people, owing to a surplus, were poorly paid.

Soon the cutting of wages began, and American foremen and workmen gradually made way for cheaper priced men. These foremen, to curry favor with the manager, have tried every means, honest or dishonest, to lessen the expenses of their departments. Among these foremen were good, bad, and indifferent men. These men do not want American workmen. One foreman was commonly quoted as saying, "I have no use for American workmen; they are too d——d independent." Complaints of the brutality of these men were carried to the central office without any redress whatever, the complainant taking the chance of discharge for so doing.

A very intelligent communication, evidently written by one in a position to know, appeared in the *Inter Ocean* about two weeks ago, by one who signed himself "Fair Play." He tells the truth and puts it very clearly. He takes the ground that the principal cause of trouble is the abuses practiced in the shops. He says:

"Here are some facts about the treatment of the men that can be easily substantiated:

"1. Certain foremen borrow money from their men, from $5 to $30, and when men complain, discharge them or lay them off.

"2. One foreman near foundry induced his men to buy lots near Burnside, by telling them the owner was a friend of Pullman and would see they were kept at work. Said foreman received commission from real estate man.

"3. One department is notorious for its drinking and profane superintendent and corps of clerks. It is a fact that they are all sometimes too "tired" to do business properly.

"4. Some of the foremen having charge of the foreign laboring classes use the vilest epithets toward them, and even attempt to kick them.

"5. All foremen who attempt to gain the good will of the men by just treatment are discharged as being, in the words of the manager, 'too good to the men.' "

In this connection I will give here a letter written to me by an employee whose name I withhold, but can produce it if necessary. He states the case clearly, and is evidently an intelligent and thoughtful man:

"REV. W. H. CARWARDINE, DEAR SIR:—In the cabinet shop (construction department), where all except laborers are employed on piece-work, the principal trouble is the reduction of prices of December last averaging thirty-three and a third per cent. Some articles were reduced as much as fifty per cent at that time.   1. Saloon doors.   Lots 2040 and 2041. Previous to August '93 prices were gradually reduced as often as a man made over the limit, which at that time was under thirty cents per hour. Cabinet-makers, at this time, were rated at from twenty to twenty-two cents per hour, for a basis to pay on account where jobs were partially completed at close of the half month.   At time of resuming work in December, cabinet-makers were rated at seventeen to nineteen cents, and prices for piece work were supposed to be made to enable men to make that rate; wherever a man made over one or two cents per hour above day rate, that particular job was again pruned in price.   2. The writer on seat ends, lot 2040, earned twenty-two cents per hour (March '94); next lot, 2041, were cut twelve and one half per cent. On the other hand, where prices were so low that some men occasionally earned less than one dollar per day, prices were not raised.   3. Mr. —————— on doors earned less than nine cents per hour.

"The prices paid for work in '93 were lower than the year previous, and the same may be said of each preceding year, so long as the writer can remember the shop, which is upwards of seven years.   In support of this may be mentioned vestibule doors, the prices of which have been revised so many times, each in the same direction, that they have ranged from $5.00 to $2.40 per pair.

"It should be noted about three fourths of the work done since last fall has been repair work on Pullman Co.'s cars, and the reduction in price has been as great on that as on contract work.

"Besides the reduction in prices, the mismanagement is apparent everywhere. The foreman has been known to set a price on a piece of work before he knew what was needed, before he saw the drawing in fact. New shelves for a folding table (M. O. 21,-176). In one case a price was set at $3.00 each for some partitions; after completion the workman made complaint of the price, which was raised to $5.00, and at this price the job paid under twenty-four cents per hour. This price was May '92. Partition E. lot 1919. Lately the foreman informed the men he no longer set prices for new work, this being done in the manager's office. During the past winter the shop has depended principally on repair work, and on this the foreman's assistants have been entrusted to fix prices. This is the result: one man gets $2.00 for scraping a door, another man receives $1.75 for the same work, and the assistant foreman paying the highest price is reprimanded, after which he endeavors to meet prices of the other petty foreman, and it is easy to see who feels this merry war.

"While in this department, during the past year the number of employees have been reduced about seventy per cent; the number of foremen and assistants remains the same. According to figures given by Mr. Wickes, rather more than one-third of the men in this department averaged for the month of April, '94, twenty cents per hour and upwards; in this one third was included the assistants of the foreman to the number of about seven. This shows how the averages of the workmen are manufactured by the Company.

"During slack times it seems an injustice some men should be kept continuously at work while others work much less than half time. Truly some are better qualified than others, and probably the Company would make such excuse; but these men who work such short time the Company think sufficient of to keep them on the pay rolls for the sake of paying rent."

Again, I will insert another letter, which tells its own sad story.

"Pullman, July 21, '94.

Rev. W. H. Carwardine.

Dear Sir:—I think it my duty to explain my case. My family consists of myself, wife and four children. We live in three small rooms with only a back entrance, for which I pay $9.00 per month, and fifty cents for water. I am considered a first-class car builder, and am a sober and industrious man and have always reported for work, whether day or piece work. I was worse off at the time of the strike by $250.00 than when I came to Pullman. In regard to wages of '93, with strict economy we barely eked out an existence, but the first part of '94 new trouble began. The Company, not satisfied, began the war by reducing our wages to a starvation point. At the time we laid down our tools, we were building a car for $19.50 that we should have got $36 for. After the second cut in our wages the stores refused to give us credit, as they knew we could not pay in full from one pay day to another. More trouble began. The Company would not give us our checks at the shops as usual, but sent us to the Company's bank, where they would have a better chance to squeeze us for the rent it was impossible to pay. I have seen myself and fellow workmen pleading with the rent agent to leave us enough to buy some member of the family a pair of shoes or some other necessity. Then when our last cut came, that was the straw that broke the camel's back; we could not stand it any longer; I, like a good many others, had to stop carrying my dinner, as what I had to carry would have run through the basket. I have seen one of my companions on the next car to mine, so weak from the lack of proper food, that he would have to rest on the way going home.

"We could see plainly it was either work and starve, or strike and depend on charity until we could win, which we are bound to do. The good Lord is always on the side of justice, and I am sure he will see justice done us.   Yours Truly."

Much complaint is made in regard to the placing of incapable men in positions of authority. Men are often placed in these positions who have no practical idea of the nature of their work. They may be adepts in something else, but not in the duties entrusted to them. Prof. Ely's criticism of ten years ago on nepotism and favoritism throws much light on these abuses.

One of the most abominable abuses practiced in these shops is that known as "blacklisting." To my own knowledge, I have seen some cruel effects of this vile practice.

One man, whose wife was an esteemed member of my church, and who himself was highly respected by all who knew him, having long held a good position in the service of the Company, was discharged for a trivial offense, and blacklisted. I am acquainted with all the details of the case. A strong temperance man, very industrious, and yet "blacklisted!" It was one of the most cruel cases of the kind I have ever known.

Fortunately for the strikers, they have a piece of splendid evidence against the Company, to prove this charge. About December, 1893, there was some trouble among the steamfitters, which resulted in the blacklisting of the following forty men. I will copy here the order, as sent out by the local manager.

Pullman, Ill., December 23, 1894.

To all Foremen: In connection with the recent trouble we have had with steamfitters, both in the construction and repair departments, I give below the names of the men who have left our employ and I hereby instruct that none of these men be employed in these works.

CONSTRUCTION DEPARTMENT.

No. 1703 Joseph Cohan.
    1705 Frank McKevilt.
    1706 William O'Meara.
    1707 James H. Matthews.
    1711 Edward Sweeney.
    1715 John Guthardt.
    1721 Martin Tracey.
    1720 Tice Mastenbrook.
    1722 Charles G. Duffy.
    1740 Frank Vincent.
    1743 Michael McNulty.
    1753 William H. Danaher.
    1764 Edward M. Barrett.
    4500 Jacob Stockman.
    4516 Robert Goebbels.
    4563 James A. Brown.
    4564 Louis Moss.
    4565 Thomas Hamilton.

Daniel J. McCarthy. ⎫
John A. Smith. ⎪
Frank Pohl. ⎬ These men were hired, but would not go to work when they found the other men had quit.
Ambrose J. Hough. ⎪
George Elwell. ⎭

REPAIR DEPARTMENT

No. 6976	Frank Engle,	Steam fitter.
6977	B. Jones,	" "
78	Thomas Johnston,	" "
80	Wm. J. Connell,	" "
83	Chas. R. McGinnis,	" "
85	C. Patton,	" "
6985	P. McCaffery,	" "
6988	Martin Craig,	" "
90	J. C. Warburton,	" "
95	B. O. Gara,	" "
7002	Josh Jones,	Helper.
7	William Mack,	"
15	Mike Carroll,	"
16	Frank Oberreich,	"
35	Dave Burrows,	"
24	M. Cunningham,	"
25	James Payne,	"
82	August Berghofer,	"

H. MIDDLETON, Manager.

Another case. A blacksmith, said to be one of the very best ever employed by the Company, left his work one afternoon for some good reason. An incipient strike took place in his absence. After the strike was over, applying for work, he found his name among the "blacklisted." Went to headquarters, manager was sorry, but could not reinstate him. Later was ordered out of his house. Still on the blacklist. I have inquired carefully into the case, and from the best authority believe it to be a case of injustice. I have his name.

This whole matter of blacklisting is worthy of Siberia. It is a disgrace to American labor. It is a boycott on labor. Capital complains of strikes and boycotts. I deprecate strikes, and I believe a boycott to be wrong, and a poor way to win good results for labor, but capital boycotts a man when she "blacklists" him. The "blacklisted" man can not only not get employment in all of the Pullman shops, and Pullman interests; but cannot even get a recommendation of good character to another employer.

A complaint of another nature comes from the Rolling Mill operatives. Why does Mr. Pullman continue the policy of refusing profitable contracts for his rolling mill—contracts for work outside of that done for the car system—and thereby keep in idleness for weeks at a time, to the detriment of their families, the best class of skilled rolling mill operatives to be found in the country? These men are mostly Englishmen, and all are splendid workmen, who make good wages while there is employment, but are idle half the time because of this peculiar policy of the Company.

It has been denied that there is political intimidation.

We all know how futile is that denial. Since the Australian ballot system came into vogue, the employees have voted about as they please, but previous to that, and at present in local elections, foremen talk very positively to their men about voting, and give them to understand what the consequences will be. I had an experience in this direction myself, in the late aldermanic election, when a certain official of the Company went to a foreman and gave him to understand that he was to withdraw his name as a candidate for a certain office, and "would in all probability be expected to settle it within that day." This roused the independence of the man, he resisted the threat and continued running for the nomination; he lost the nomination, but defeated the chances of the Company's candidate. The candidate opposed by the Company was elected. In a few weeks, the independent foreman was asked to resign. He had been years in the employ of the Company, and was one of its most efficient men. Two other employees interested in his candidacy were also asked to resign. Theoretically the Pullman Company never interferes with the politics of its employees, but practically there have been strong evidences the other way.

There is absolutely no recognition of merit in the policy of the Company. Changes are constant. A peculiarity of the town of Pullman is the evanescent character of its life. It seems to be inherent in the system. Many men remain in the employ of the company for years; but no one is safe. There is a constant feeling of insecurity. Men have put in years of hard, laborious work, only to be dismissed without a moment's warning, and then scarcely to receive a word of thanks. This is the strangest thing to me in the whole system. I have been surprised to see how quick, and on what slight ground faithful men are discharged.

In such a vast system, perfection is impossible, and injustice may be occasionally done without intent. But there is no reason why true merit should not be appreciated and encouraged. Such a Company as this can afford to be generous and sincere in its treatment of its men. Promotion and recognition is reciprocal in its effect. Nothing is lost thereby. And in this connection we might add that the pensioning of its old and tried employees is an unknown factor in the daily life of this Company.

Again, the Company is greatly enriched by inventions of its employees, for which they give the employee neither money nor credit. Many ingenious inventions and devices are scattered throughout the shops that bring in good returns, but not to their inventors. Mr. Pullman, said to be one of the greatest inventors of the age, instead of encouraging a spirit of invention among his employees, and giving them the credit thereof, on the contrary, enforces the law upon them, by which, if they do invent anything in his shops, they shall relinquish all title to the same.

A grievous charge made by the employees against those in authority in the shops is that of personal abuse. Foul and abusive language on the part of a foreman or the head of a department, or even by an official, should not be tolerated for a moment. I do

not wonder that men whose wages have been reduced to such a low ebb, should retaliate when insult and abuse is added to low wages. I well remember, when an orphan boy in the city of New York,
having to work for six years under an abusive foreman in the composing room of the *New York
Evening Post*. Of all the men I have ever met, he
was the embodiment of tyranny. A man of considerable ability, but foul in language and despotic in
authority, the daily terror of all who were under his
influence. He treated men like dogs, swore at them
and abused them without stint. In those days there
was engendered in my soul a hatred against tyrannical foremen and abusive treatment of men which
has never left me, and which during the past months
of our long and sad winter, made my very blood boil
with indignation at what I have seen and heard.
Then it was that I declared if ever the opportunity
presented itself to defend the true rights of laboring
men, and smite those who unmercifully oppressed
them, I would lift up my voice and cry aloud, in the
name of the God of Israel.

One other charge of selfish evasion of duty I would
prefer against this great Pullman Palace Car Company is that it does not give damages unless absolutely compelled to, to those who are injured or die
in its service.

There are numerous cases in the town of Pullman
illustrative of this. A lady whose husband had long

been in the employ of the Company, is now a widow.
Her husband died from the effects of the breakage of
the machine on which he was working, the name of
which I will not mention for fear of injuring her
case. She has been making every effort to get a
settlement from the Company for many months. But
procrastination and evasions have met her at every
turn, until now she is heartily discouraged.

The public will doubtless remember the case of
the colored porter who had been seriously injured
in the service of the Company, and applied repeatedly
for satisfaction. At last when McPherson, the Company's lawyer, secured a strap from him in the Company's city offices, the best evidence he had, in sheer
desperation he turned and fired three shots from a
revolver, neither of them producing any serious
damage.

Many cases might be enumerated showing how a
great and wealthy corporation resorts to every possible method to avoid settling claims of those who
have a right to receive help from them.

Pitiful are the stories told of the sick and injured
who receive little or no compensation for injuries
done. There is an official Doctor and Surgeon, who
gives a certain amount of medical service to the
injured. It used to be that a sick man was allowed
for a certain time $2.00 a day; then gradually it was
reduced to $1.00 a day, and that only paid when he
could report for work and pick up screws from a heap

of different sized screws on the floor.

I will conclude this point with the quotation of a letter giving a statement of the treatment by the Company of a certain Mrs. Wood, a member of my church, whose husband died as the result of wounds inflicted while in the performance of duty as a watchman. She is responsible for her own statement. The case is a well known one in Pullman and created great interest at the time. The writer says:

"Buckley Wood, of 312 Stephenson Street, watchman at the Fulton Street gate, was assaulted July 15, 1886, by a man named Pearson, who tried to take a box of tools through the outer gate without a pass, which was required by the rules of the Company, and which Mr. Wood asked for, when Pearson struck him in the face with a hatchet, knocking out two of his teeth and knocking him down so that he fell striking the back of his head on a stone. He was unable to give an account of the assault for over a week.

"Pearson was arrested by a policeman named Thos. Kane, and was locked up in the Kensington Station until transferred to Hyde Park. When the case was called, Mr. Wood was not able to appear, and policeman Kane prevailed upon Mrs. Wood not to leave her husband to attend the trial, as the police would see to it that justice was done, which they did by letting the defense choose the jury, which brought in a verdict of 'not guilty.' They held that Mr. Wood had no right to stop Pearson from taking his own tools from the shops. In which case I think the Pullman Company should have been responsible, inasmuch as they gave him strict orders not to allow any one to take anything from the shops without a pass from their foreman. Police Captain Hunt went with

Mrs. Wood and witnesses to the city to get an indictment for the man, but when they arrived the grand jury had adjourned for six weeks, and when they returned, Pearson, having been notified of their intentions through some source, had decamped for parts unknown, until it was learned he was arrested and convicted, and sent to state prison for two years in the state of Ohio for assaulting an old man about a year afterward.

"Mr. Wood was employed afterward in the Paint department, not through kindness of the Pullman Company, but rather that of Mr. Thomas Kennedy, who was then superintendent of the paint department, and knew that Mr. Wood was not really able to do any work. He let him put in his time doing any little odd jobs he could do; as the Pullman Company did not consider him as being in good enough health to resume his position as watchman, and the books of the Pullman Company will show how many, many days he was not even able to walk to the shop, as through the kindness of Mr. Kennedy, if he once got to the shop, he was not compelled to do any work as long as the higher officials did not see him doing nothing. In that way he lived until the 30th of May following, when he died as surely from the effect of his injuries of the previous July as if he had died the same day.

"Mrs. Wood, thinking it altogether useless for a poor widow to try and fight a corporation like the Pullman Company, did not act on advice she received from many friends to bring suit against them, but tried to make some arrangement with Mr. Sessions, then manager of the works in Pullman, whereby she could have the use of the house in which she lived, but he said he had no authority to let her have the house without paying rent for it. She wrote several times, once through her minister, pastor of the first

M. E. church, who registered a letter to Mr. Pullman, but did not receive an answer. She decided to pay the rent and did so, with the exception of six weeks' rent($26.56)at the time of her husband's death, which they gave her as a free gift in recompense for the life of her husband. At three different times since, when she has been unable to meet the rent bills promptly, she has had notice of eviction, and been compelled to borrow enough money to pay the rent to keep from having her goods put out into the street, once in December, 1893, when she had got behind in the rent, but made arrangements with the town agent to pay the old rent as she could, and let her daughter take the responsibility of the house from January 1, 1894. She did, and paid a rental of $17.-71 per month from a salary of $1.00 (one dollar) per day, having the remainder to support herself and mother. The January rent she paid cash and for February, March and April she paid it from her pay checks, paying for the four months rent $70.84 and receiving in payment not over $25.00 above rent for the same four months. On the third of May it seems that after Miss Wood had been out of work over a week they made the startling discovery that they had credited $12.71 (which she had paid in January)to the account of the old bill (with which she had no connection, as she paid her board until January 1), but instead of correcting their mistake, gave her notice to vacate the house on the 3rd of May, for a bill of $12.71 due on January rent, while she held receipts for February, March and April, and when she remonstrated in the Pullman bank the clerk said he had credited it as he saw fit and would not change it, and she would be compelled to pay it over or leave the house.

"Mrs. Wood told the agent she would go to headquarters, when he flew into a passion, and told her if she dared go to Mr. Wickes she would be made to suffer for it. She did go to see Mr. Wickes, who told her that something should have been done for her before if he had known of her case, of which he claimed he knew nothing. He told her she should go home and rest contented, that she would not be troubled. Mr. Middleton, the present manager of the works, told her that her daughter would not be troubled for the rent, that she should draw what money was coming to her; after which, on May 21st, ten days after the strike, when she went to draw the money due her, $3.53, she was asked to sign it over for rent, which she refused to do and does not know whether or not she will be compelled to move for non-payment of rent when the strike is over."

Now, in view of these facts, the great true-hearted public, believers in fair play, will see that it is not all sunshine in Pullman. This great undercurrent of dissatisfaction, culminating in the strike of May 11th, had some underlying causes back of it. Some of the things I have mentioned may seem trivial, but like the lesser streams emptying into the greater, and swelling the impetus thereof, so these countless lesser abuses and tyrannies have wrought out their awful and disastrous results. How long will great corporations continue to deal thus inhumanly with employees?

I do not and never have hesitated to place the responsibility of the strike upon the Company. The public must bear in mind that while the action of the employees seemed hasty, still they had great cause for action. To say that it was produced entirely by the "labor agitator" is to insult the intelligence of the finest body of mechanics gathered together in any one place in the United States. I contend that when a body of men such as we have here, lay down their tools and leave the work bench, as did these men, that they are actuated by some great underlying motive, and that it will not do to call them idiots and fools.

These employees were in a very sensitive and suspicious state of mind. A long winter, with its countless causes for grievance and dissatisfaction, was just behind them. They had been so ground between the upper mill stone of "low wages" and the nether mill stone of "high rents," the continued oppression of the "straw bosses," the smothered but still unsuppressed dislike of the general and local management, which has added to rather than sought to alleviate their troubles, and a system of surveillance that seems to be indigenous to the very atmosphere of the place, that they were in no condition to be trifled with by the Company.

CHAPTER X.

Suffer a few words of personal allusion. When I delivered my sermon on "The Pullman Strike," ten days after its employees walked out of the shops, I had no idea that it would have created the interest that it has.

It was rather an audacious act to perform, because, owing to the peculiarity of the paternalistic government of Pullman, no one feels like openly criticising the Company. The time having arrived, I spoke out, what were my honest, candid convictions, without thought of fear or favor. My position was peculiar. I did not endorse the strike, and never have. I did not endorse the boycott. Repeatedly have I said this. But I stood for justice. If the workingmen believe in strikes and boycotts, all right. They have found that strikes may do, but boycotts will not do. But these working men use the weapons seemingly most useful, as they think, for their purpose. But I look back of all this, and say, "Let us unearth the cause!" Strike at the root. Don't revile and curse these employees! Vituperation of strikers will do no good. Study the situation, and give them in their demand for justice your sympathy and moral support. Stir up one

118

half of society to behold the wrongs of the other half. If you have a theory that will solve their problem, bring it forth, and let them see it—don't cry anarchy and run away from them, or leave them to the tender mercies of the militia and the police.

Quell the mobs—shoot all law-breakers in time of awful peril. But do not call all "strikers" anarchists.

Holding this position, I was surprised to find how the fear of anarchy and mob rule blinded the eyes of true men and women to the injustice that had wrought all these things. We had better look at the evil calmly, and remedy it; or the evil in the future will break forth again in awful fury, with far more disastrous results. I have found my position has not been altogether a pleasant one. While I am commended on all sides by the better classes, who daily deluge me with letters, interviews, questions, etc., and while I am regarded with infinite kindness by the striking employees, still I find plenty who are ready to chide me.

I must not forget here to acknowledge with greatful appreciation the sympathy and co-operation of my beloved friend and brother pastor, the Rev. Wilbur F. Atchison, pastor of the Hyde Park M. E. Church, and his talented wife, Mrs. Rena-Michaels Atchison, formerly Dean of the Women's College at Evanston, and now Secretary of the State Woman's Suffrage Society of Illinois. In them I have found true sympathy for the cause of the laborer.

We have fallen on serious times.

The inequalities of life as indicated in the social fabric of modern society are simply fearful. In many respects we are living in the grandest age this old world has ever seen. And yet, with our boasted progress and advancement, I realize that something is radically wrong in a condition of society that permits some to be so poor and others to be so rich. It certainly looks as though the poor were growing poorer and the rich becoming richer.

No person who has ever read Sir Walter Scott's wonderful story of "Ivanhoe" can forget the picture of Gurth, the Swineherd. Describing him, Scott says: "One part of his dress only remains, but it is too remarkable to be suppressed. It was a brass ring, resembling a dog's collar, but without any opening, and soldered fast round his neck, so loose as to form no impediment to his breathing, yet so tight as to be incapable of being removed excepting by the use of the file. On this singular gorget was engraven in Saxon characters an inscription of the following purport: 'Gurth, the son of Beowulph, is the born thrall of Cedric of Rotherwood.'"

What a picture!

What a change to-day!

And yet, while we have moved some little distance from the day that lives again in the glowing pages of Sir Walter, nevertheless Gurth, the son of Beowulph, is with us yet.

While he wears not the collar of Cedric of Rotherwood, yet he is to all intents and purposes the chattel or "White Slave," of the "corporation," "trust" or "millionaire lords," many of whom it may be said are in these days of growing social inequality, the Cedrics of Rotherwood of modern society.

We as a nation are dividing ourselves, like ancient Rome, into two classes, the rich and the poor, the oppressor and the oppressed. And on the side of the oppressor there is power and protection, class legislation and military support. Should this policy continue for a generation or two, there can be no doubt at all that working men who in times of war and invasion are the protectors of our liberties and homes, would refuse to take up arms in their defense. We are following in the tracks of ancient Rome, instead of learning useful lessons from her failures and defeats. No country can prosper, no government long perpetuate itself and its institutions, which does not administer judgment and justice alike to all of its people. Napoleon said God was always on the side of the heaviest battalions, but God Himself has said that He is on the side of righteousness and justice for the poor and needy, and that He will avenge their cause against the oppressor.

The oppressed of to-day are white laborers and mechanics who, evidently, though without a Supreme Court decision, have no rights which millionaires and moneyed corporations are bound to respect. And with the oppressor there is power. But as is invariably the case, proven by ancient and modern history, the oppressor is the heaviest loser. Men and nations sometimes oppress to their own hurt. An estimate of the *money* losses in the present strike up to July 9, '94, puts them at $6,560,500, of which the laborers have lost in wages $1,500,000. And this does not include the loss to the business and commerce of the country, nor the cost to the federal and state governments of the military occupation. And all this grows out of the oppression of one man who was once a poor mechanic. He has gained wealth, and risen into power on it so that he can now take advantage of the necessities and poverty of his fellowmen to crush and oppress them.

Whatever the fathers who organized this government intended it to be, we, their successors, have evidently drifted very far away from the original intention of the founders. It is no longer a government of equal rights for all. The present strike may be overcome by federal bayonets and bullets, but the trouble will not end here. There is deep unrest in the lowest strata of society, the real burden-bearers of our country, which augurs ill for capitalistic oppression in the future. The United States is to be the theater for the presentation of the best possible results of human government. We are giving an object lesson in government to the world. And these results are to be developed within a very few years, too. I therefore deprecate, though necessary, the use of federal troops in this strike as a precedent, pregnant with evil in years to come. Capital seems to be organized to destroy the independence of labor and defeat its efforts at elevation; and labor is organized not only to protect itself, but to retaliate on capital. These conditions can not be perpetuated. One force or other must yield or be destroyed, or a common ground of reconciliation must be found for both.

Can there not be found a common ground of agreement between capital and labor? If they are to exist at all, they must live as husband and wife, each the counterpart of the other, each for the other's interests and welfare. My suggestion is that there should be National and State Courts of Arbitration; the former in cases of appeal, reviewing the decisions of the latter, and having final jurisdiction in all cases whether of review or original. I say *courts*, not committees of inquiry. If international disputes can be thus settled, why should not national or local be? The strong arm of the law should compel the autocratic millionaire as well as the dependent mechanic to submit his case and abide by the decision. And where, as in this strike, there is an obstinate refusal to arbitrate, then the federal or state governments should take possession of the railroads, the telegraph, the coal mines, or the manufacturing plants, and run them in the interest of the whole people, and not in the interest of obstinate corporations. The public good and the peace of the country demand this.

The man or body of men, corporation or labor union which refuses to arbitrate their differences are traitors to their country's best interests, violators of her laws, instigators to riot, and enemies of every principle that is good and pure and holy and peaceable. They should be dealt with to the utmost extent and with utmost rigor of the law.

Among other lessons impressed upon the mind of the American people by the great crisis through which we have narrowly passed, is that of the power and dangers of combined labor, the inhumanity of corporations, the unrest of society, the necessity of some new legislation, and the expediency of independent political action.

I appeal to the great body of the laboring classes, in view of the developments of the past few weeks, hereafter and forever to use your ballot aright. It is the God-given privilege of every American citizen, purchased at the sacrifice of blood, tears and property, and which is the birthright of 4,000 years of slow and painful evolution from degradation, slavery and tyranny to the liberty of this latter nineteenth century. A ballot unknown in ancient days, in the Mosaic economy, and Roman history; a ballot that first began to make its appearance when the Barons at Runnymede demanded the rights of Magna Charta from King John of England, when Oliver Cromwell rose against the despotism of Charles I , with his Star Chamber, and when Martin Luther blew a blast that awoke all Europe to the dawn of the Reformation; a ballot that was not born until the urgent demands of a home government once more created a rebellion, and the American Colonies were established, and that masterpiece of human composition, the Declaration of Independence, given to the world; a ballot, forsooth, that did not reach its majority until Abraham Lincoln broke the manacles that enslaved 3,000,-000 black men, and signed that Magna Charta of human liberty, the Act of Emancipation; a ballot that represents a government of the people, by the people, and for the people, free homes, free schools, free press, a united people, the right of every man unmolested to worship God according to the dictates of his own conscience; the greatest gift given by God to man outside of his blessed Son, our Lord and Savior Jesus Christ, and one that can give us, if we use it right, the grandest type of government under the sun!

O, workmen of America, use this gift aright, for principle, not party, for men who are patriots and who are able to represent your best interest! Love your country. There is no better in this world. Love and uphold our constitution, and ever protect the flag for which our fathers, *my father*, died.

Go forth, little book, like a piece of driftwood tossed out on the watery main of life, and may God's blessing go with you. You have been written in the true spirit of my blessed Master, who scourged when it was necessary, whose soul burned with heated indignation against the oppressors of the poor, who compared false prophets to whited sepulchers, and yet who spoke words of loving kindness to the downtrodden, and helped to smooth the weary way of life to burdened souls. Yours has been a labor of love. May you reach the homes of wealth, and awaken them to their duty, may you fire the hearts of reformers to greater deeds, may you stir the minds of legislators to the need of better laws, and may you, above all, help to bring the great mass of the laboring millions to realize that the secret of their greatest happiness and the settlement of all our industrial troubles lies in the upholding of the true principles of that Christianity, irrespective of creed, which was given to the world by Him who not only said, "Do unto others as ye would that they should do unto you," but also that

The Laborer is Worthy of His Hire.

THE END.